For Engineers & Designers

TurboCAD Exercises

200 3D PRACTICE DRAWINGS

SACHIDANAND JHA

©Copyright 2019 CADIN360, All rights reserved

Dear Reader,

Thank you for choosing **TurboCAD Exercises** book. This book is part of a family of premium-quality CADIN360 books, all of which are written by Outstanding author who combine practical experience with a gift for teaching.

CADIN360 was founded in 2016. More than 3 years later, we're still committed to producing consistently exceptional books. With each of our titles, we're working hard to set a new standard for the industry. From the paper we print on, to the authors we work with, our goal is to bring you the best books available.

I hope you see all that reflected in these pages. I'd be very interested to hear your comments and get your feedback on how we're doing. Feel free to let me know what you think about this or any other CADIN360 book by sending me an email at contactus@cadin360.com.

If you think you've found a technical error in this book, please visit
https://cadin360.com/contact-us/.
Customer feedback is critical to our efforts at CADIN360.

Best regards,

Sachidanand Jha
Founder & CEO, CADIN360

TurboCAD Exercises

Published by
CADIN360
cadin360.com
Copyright © 2019 by CADIN360, All rights reserved.

This book is copyrighted and the CADIN360 reserves all rights.
No part of this publication may be reproduced, stored in a retrieval system or transmitted, transcribed, stored in retrieval system or translated into any language, in any form or by any means, electronic, mechanical, photocopying, recording, scanning or otherwise, without the prior written permission of the publisher & Author.

Limit of Liability/Disclaimer of Warranty:
The publisher and the author make no representations or warranties with respect to the accuracy or completeness of the contents of this work and specifically disclaim all warranties, including without limitation warranties of fitness for a particular purpose. No warranty may be created or extended by sales or promotional materials. The advice and strategies contained herein may not be suitable for every situation. This work is sold with the understanding that the publisher is not engaged in rendering legal, accounting, or other professional services. If professional assistance is required, the services of a competent professional person should be sought. Neither the publisher nor the author shall be liable for damages arising herefrom. The fact that an organization or Web site is referred to in this work as a citation and/or a potential source of further information does not mean that the author or the publisher endorses the information the organization or Web site may provide or recommendations it may make. Further, readers should be aware that Internet Web sites listed in this work may have changed or disappeared between when this work was written and when it is read.

Examination Copies
Books received as examination copies in any form such as paperback and eBook are for review only and may not be made available for the use of the student. These files may not be transferred to any other party. Resale of examination copies is prohibited

Electronic Files
The electronic file/eBook in any form of this book is licensed to the original user only and may not be transferred to any other party.

Disclaimer:
All trademarks and registered trademarks appearing in this book are the property of their respective owners.

Preface

TurboCAD Exercises

❖ This book contain 200 CAD practice exercises and drawings.

❖ This book does not provide step by step tutorial to design 3D models.

❖ S.I Unit is used.

❖ Predominantly used Third Angle Projection.

❖ This book is for **TurboCAD** and Other Feature-Based Modeling Software such as Inventor, SolidWorks, NX, Solid Edge, AutoCAD, PTC Creo etc.

❖ It is intended to provide Drafters, Designers and Engineers with enough 3D CAD exercises for practice on **TurboCAD**.

❖ It includes almost all types of exercises that are necessary to provide, clear, concise and systematic information required on industrial machine part drawings.

❖ Third Angle Projection is intentionally used to familiarize Drafters, Designers and Engineers in Third Angle Projection to meet the expectation of world wide Engineering drawing print.

❖ Clear and well drafted drawing help easy understanding of the design.

❖ This book is for Beginner, Intermediate and Advance CAD users.

❖ These exercises are from Basics to Advance level.

❖ Each exercises can be assigned and designed separately.

❖ No Exercise is a prerequisite for another. All dimensions are in mm.

❖ Note: Assume any missing dimensions.

©Copyright 2019 CADIN360, All rights reserved

EX-01

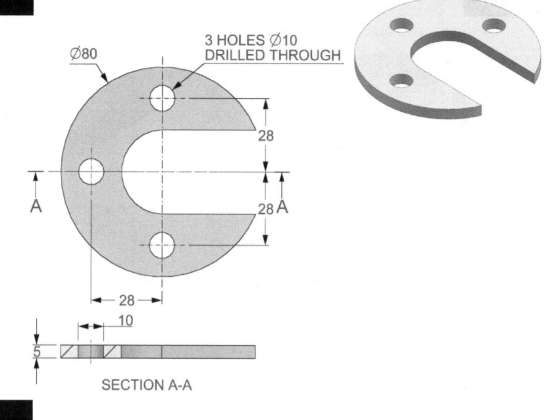

Ø80

3 HOLES Ø10
DRILLED THROUGH

28

28 A

A

28

10

5

SECTION A-A

EX-02

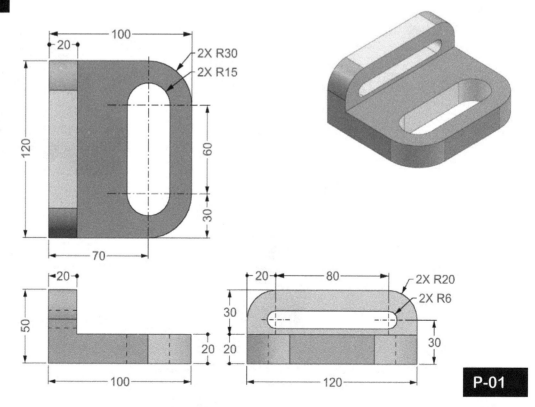

100

20

2X R30

2X R15

120

60

30

70

20

50

20 20

100

20

80

2X R20

2X R6

30

30

120

P-01

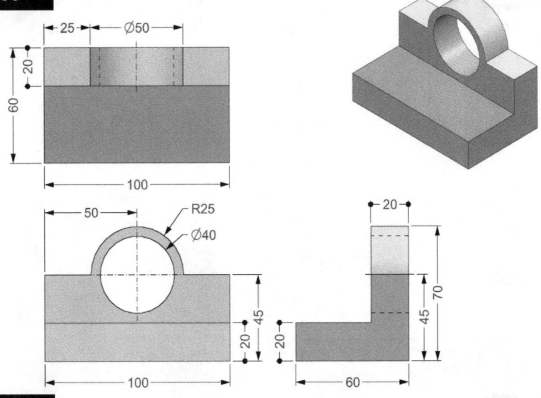

25 — Ø50

20

60

100

50 — R25
Ø40

45
20
20

20
70
45
60

Ø40

30

30

Ø20

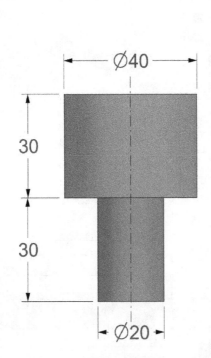

EX-05

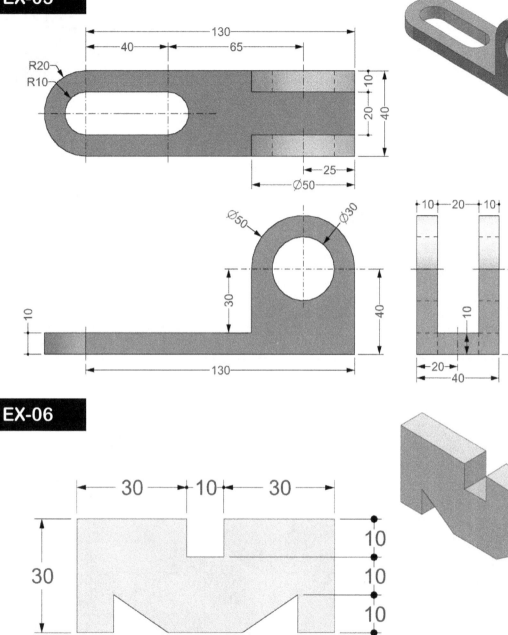

EX-06

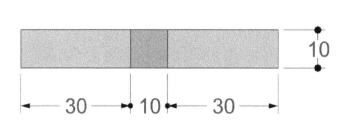

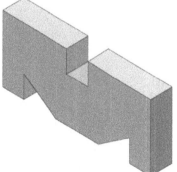

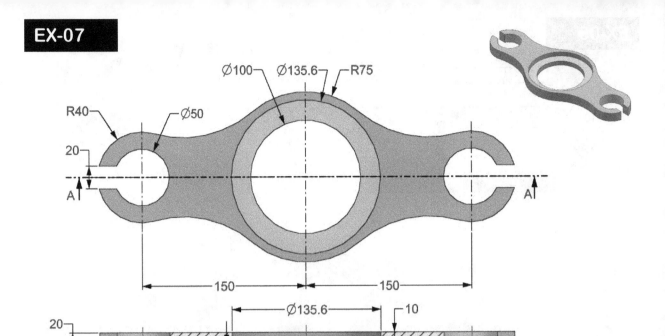

SECTION A-A
(SCALE 1:1)

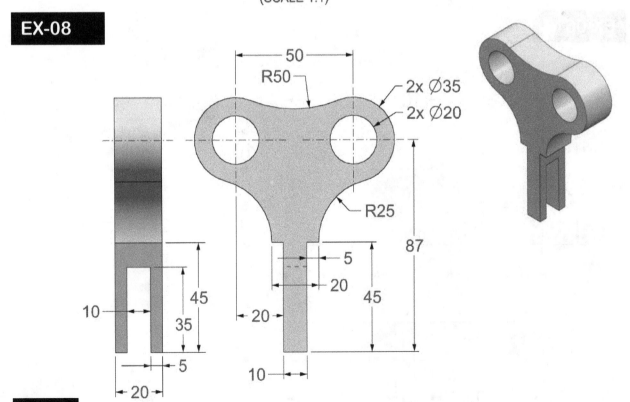

EX-09

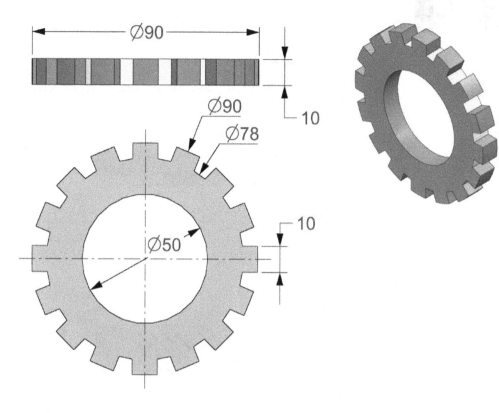

⌀90

10

⌀90
⌀78
⌀50
10

EX-10

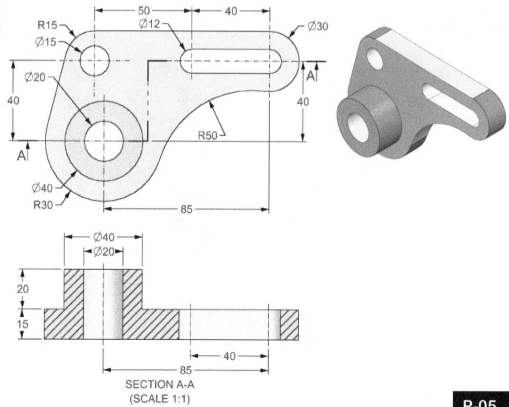

50
40
R15
⌀12
⌀30
⌀15
⌀20
A
40
40
R50
R30
⌀40
85

⌀40
⌀20
20
15
40
85

SECTION A-A
(SCALE 1:1)

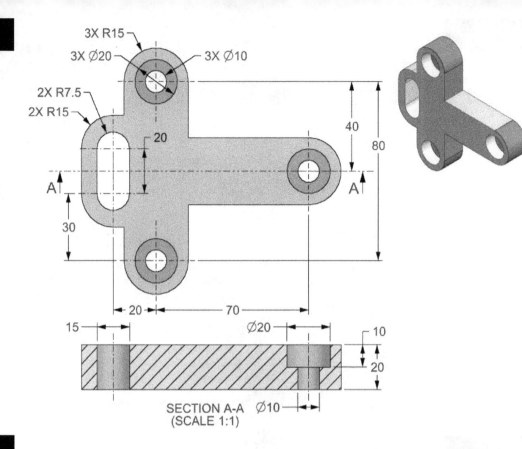

3X R15
3X Ø20
3X Ø10
2X R7.5
2X R15
20
40
80
A
30
20
70
15
Ø20
10
20
SECTION A-A
(SCALE 1:1)
Ø10

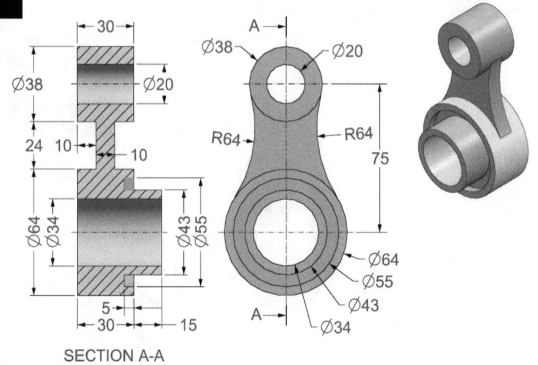

30
Ø38
Ø20
24   10
10
Ø64
Ø34
Ø43
Ø55
5
30
15

A
Ø38
Ø20
R64
R64
75
Ø64
Ø55
Ø43
Ø34
A

SECTION A-A
(SCALE 1:1)

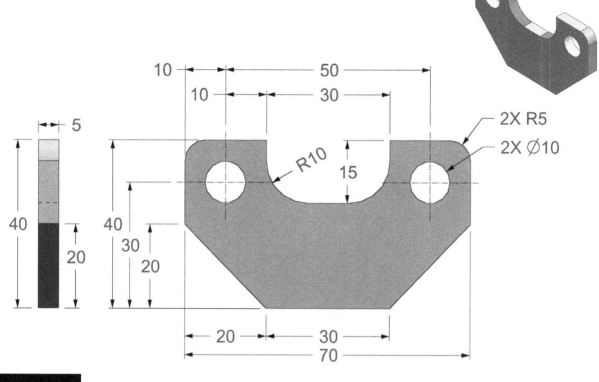

2X R5
2X ∅10
R10
10
10
50
30
5
15
40
40
30
20
20
20
30
70

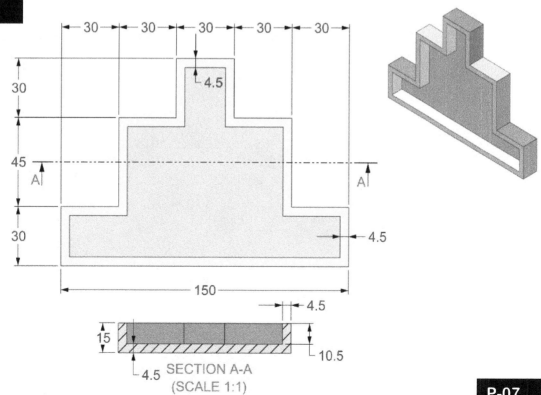

30   30   30   30   30
30
4.5
45
A| |A
30
4.5
150
4.5
15
10.5
4.5   SECTION A-A
(SCALE 1:1)

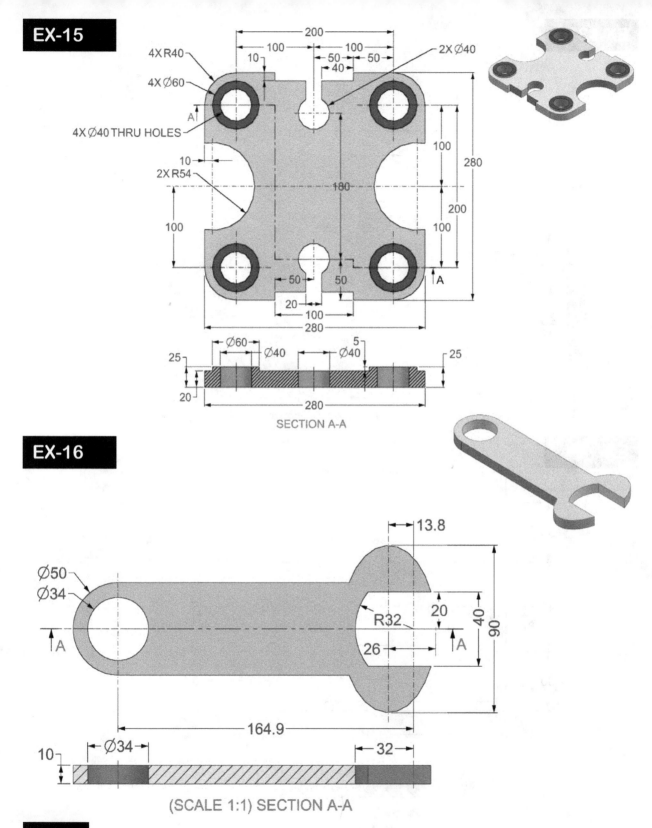

EX-15

4X R40
4X Ø60
4X Ø40 THRU HOLES
200
100
100
10
50
50
40
2X Ø40
10
2X R54
180
280
100
200
100
100
100
50
50
20
100
280

Ø60
Ø40
5
Ø40
25
25
20
280

SECTION A-A

EX-16

Ø50
Ø34
13.8
20
40
90
R32
26
A
A
164.9

Ø34
32
10
(SCALE 1:1) SECTION A-A

P-08

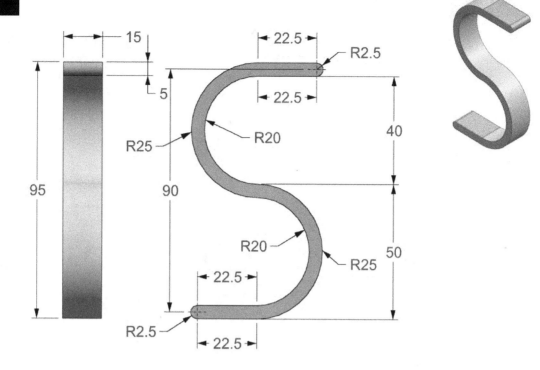

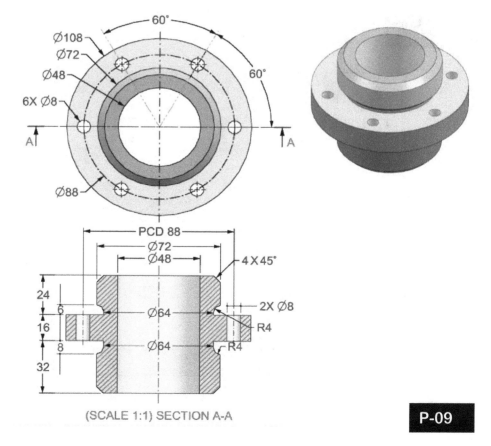

(SCALE 1:1) SECTION A-A

EX-19

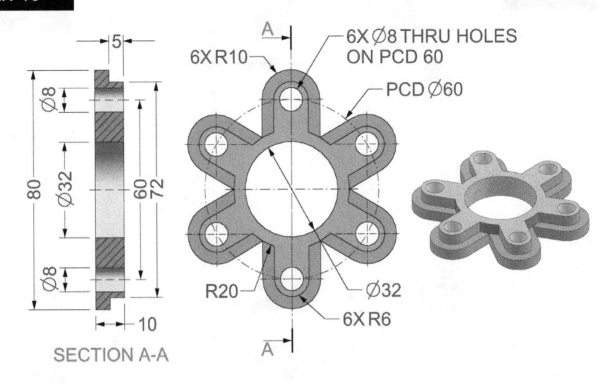

6X R10

6X Ø8 THRU HOLES
ON PCD 60

PCD Ø60

Ø8

Ø32

60

72

80

R20

Ø32

6X R6

10

5

SECTION A-A

A

A

EX-20

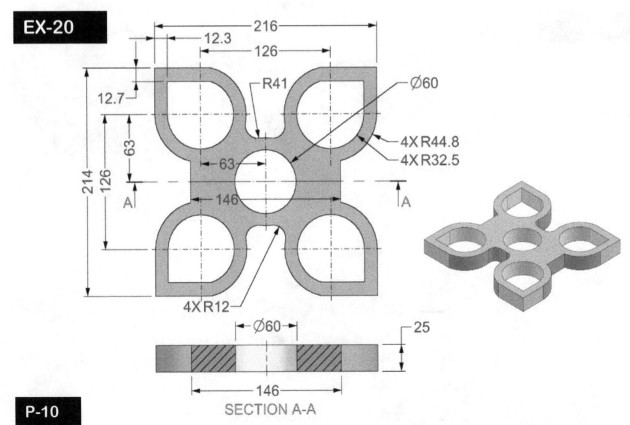

216

12.3

126

12.7

R41

Ø60

4X R44.8
4X R32.5

63

63

214

126

146

A

A

4X R12

Ø60

25

146

SECTION A-A

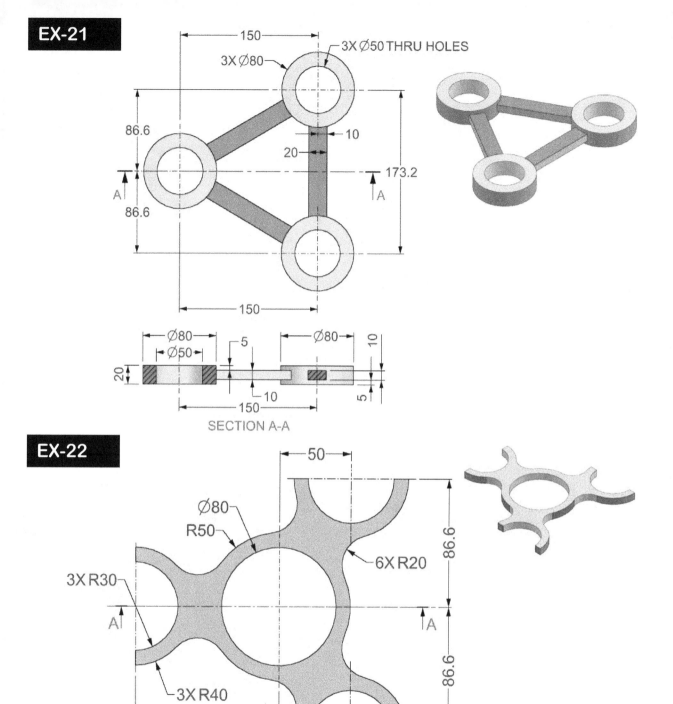

EX-21

150

3X Ø50 THRU HOLES

3X Ø80

86.6

10

20

173.2

86.6

A

A

150

Ø80

Ø50

5

20

10

10

Ø80

10

5

150

SECTION A-A

EX-22

50

Ø80

R50

86.6

6X R20

3X R30

A

A

86.6

3X R40

100

50

10

Ø80

SECTION A-A

P-11

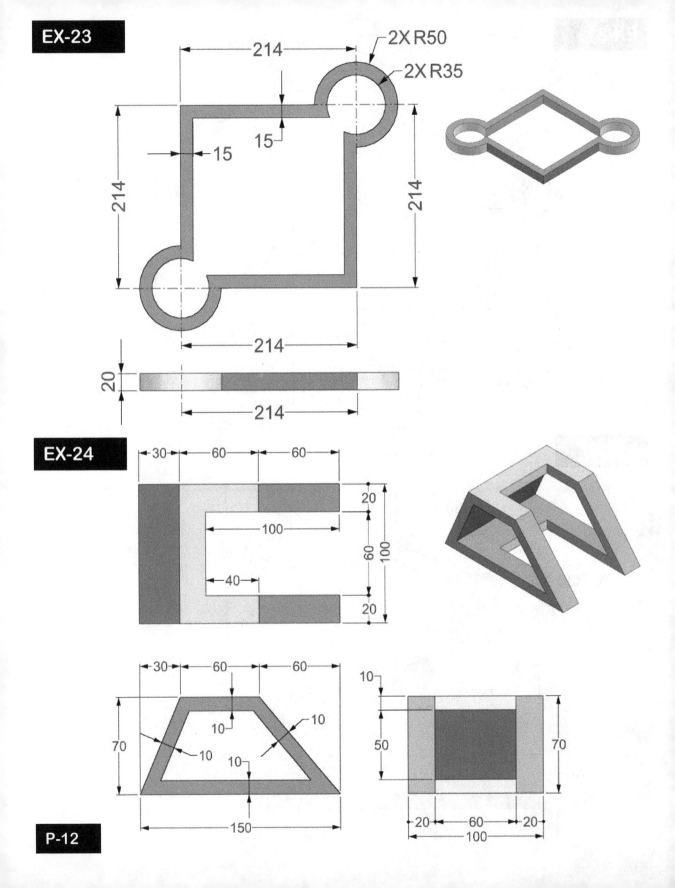

EX-23

214

2X R50

2X R35

15

15

214

214

214

20

214

EX-24

30 60 60

20

100

60 100

40

20

P-12

30 60 60

10

10

70

10

10

10

150

10

50

70

20 60 20

100

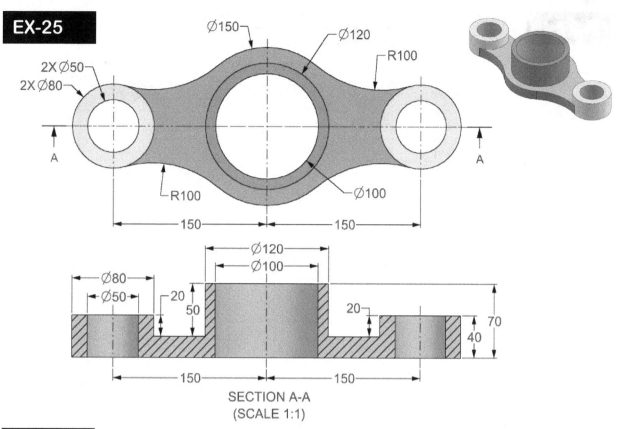

EX-25

∅150
∅120
R100
2X ∅50
2X ∅80
R100
∅100
150 150

∅120
∅100
∅80
∅50
20
50
20
70
40
150 150

SECTION A-A
(SCALE 1:1)

EX-26

∅24
∅44
∅36

∅44
∅36
∅32
∅24
2X45°
12
4
8 36
3
12

SECTION A-A
(SCALE 1:1)

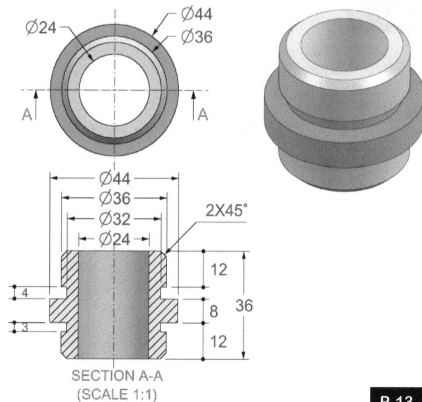

EX-27

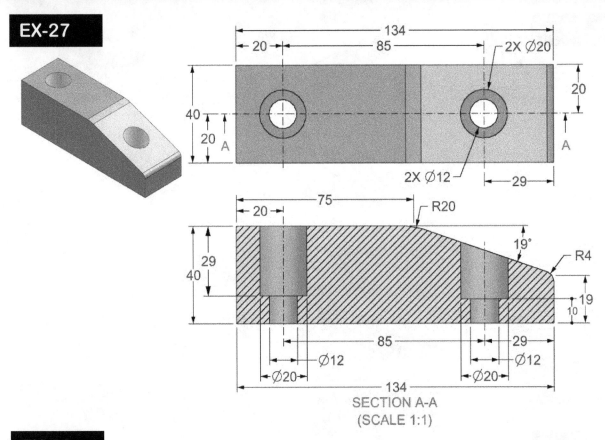

134
20
85
2X Ø20
20
40
20
A
2X Ø12
29
A

SECTION A-A
(SCALE 1:1)

75
20
R20
19°
R4
29
40
19
10
85
29
Ø12
Ø20
Ø12
Ø20
134

EX-28

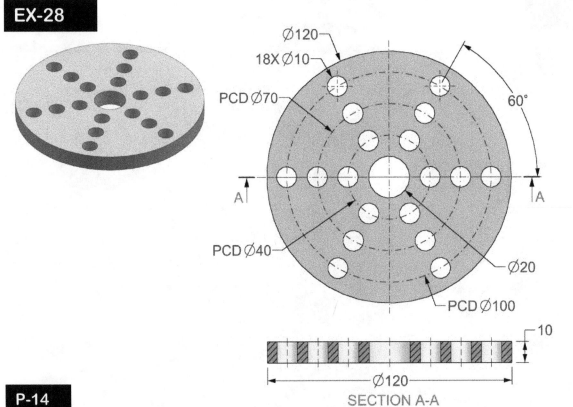

Ø120
18X Ø10
PCD Ø70
60°
PCD Ø40
Ø20
PCD Ø100
10
Ø120

SECTION A-A

EX-29

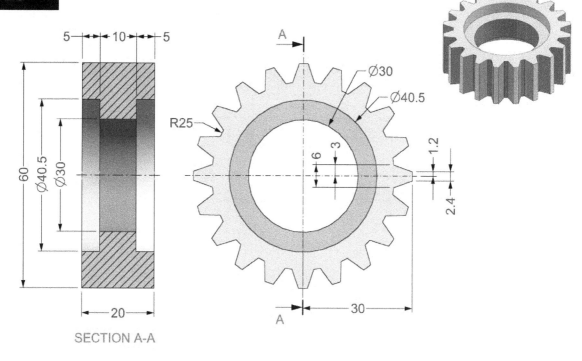

SECTION A-A

EX-30

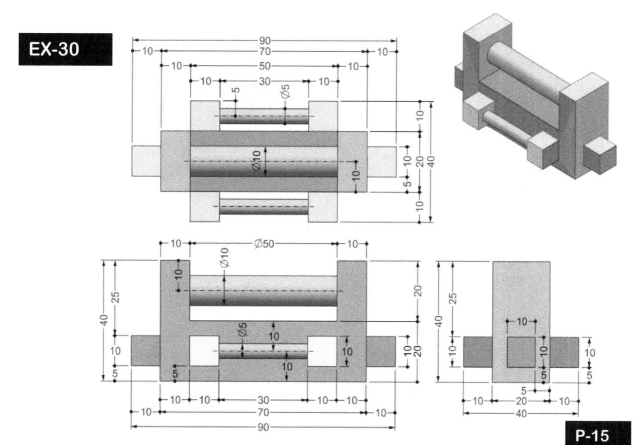

EX-31

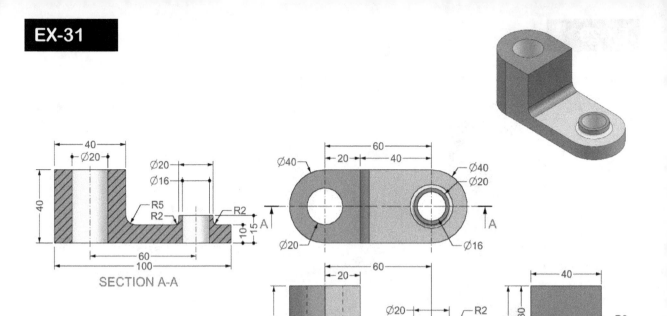

SECTION A-A

EX-32

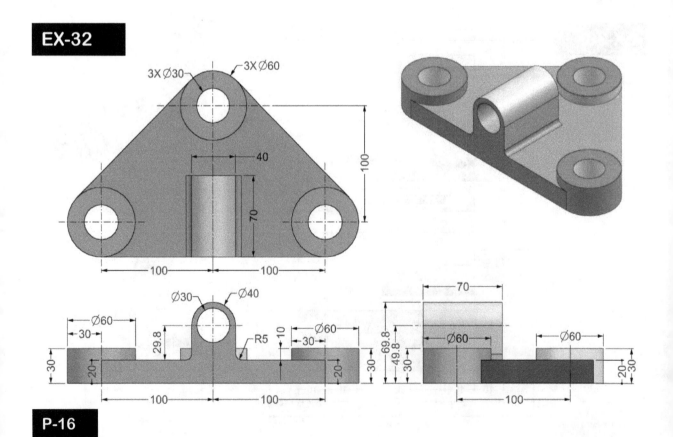

P-16

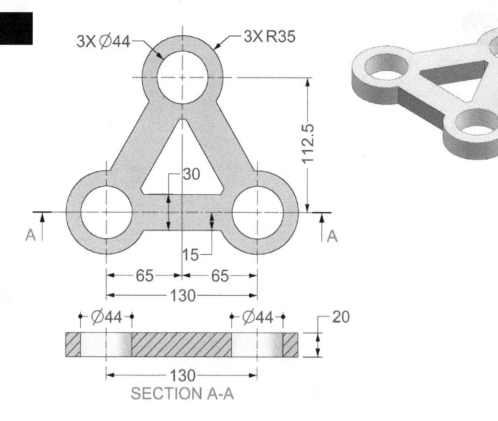

3X Ø44   3X R35

112.5

30

15

A   A

65   65

130

Ø44   Ø44   20

130

SECTION A-A

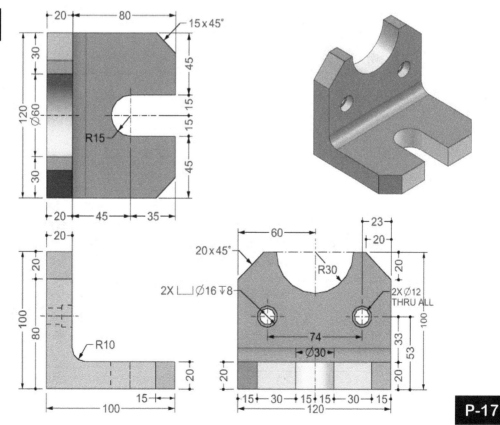

20   80   15 x 45°

30

45

120   15 15

Ø60   15

R15   15

30   45

20   45   35

20

20

100   80

R10

20

100   15

60   23

20 x 45°   20

R30   20

2X ⌴ Ø16 ↧8   2X Ø12 THRU ALL

74   100

Ø30   33

53

20   20

15 30 15 15 30 15

120

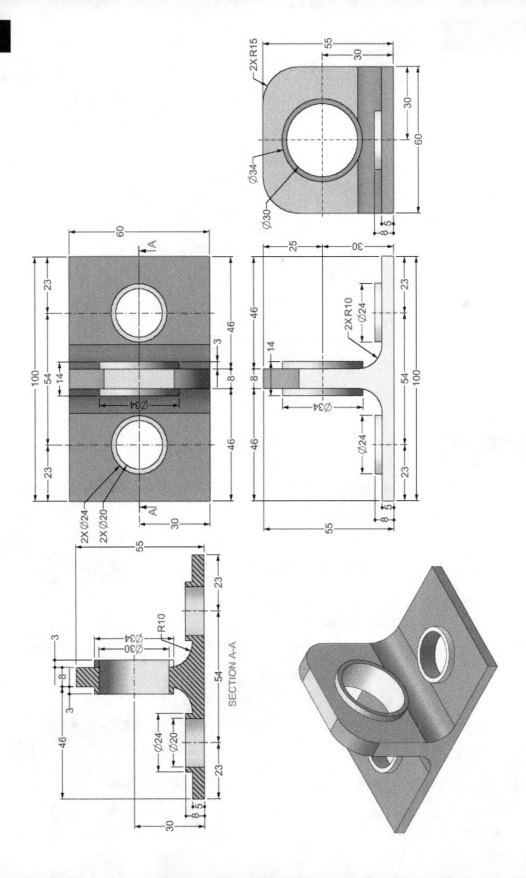

SECTION A-A

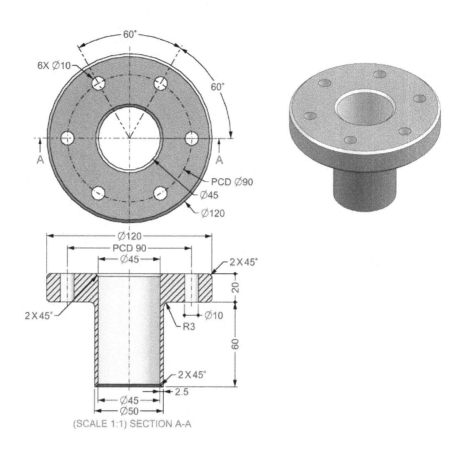

60°

6X Ø10

60°

PCD Ø90

Ø45

Ø120

Ø120

PCD 90

Ø45

2 X 45°

20

2 X 45°

Ø10

R3

60

2 X 45°

2.5

Ø45

Ø50

(SCALE 1:1) SECTION A-A

A   A

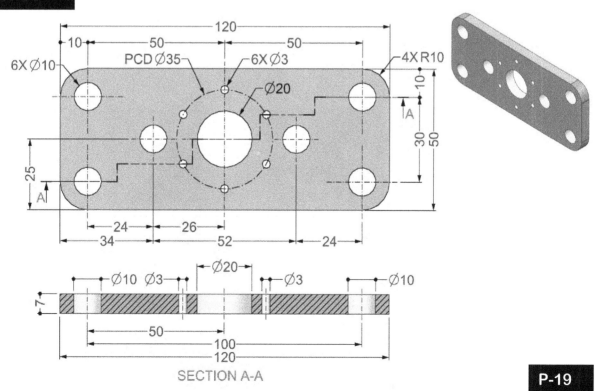

120

10   50   50

6X Ø10   PCD Ø35   6X Ø3   4X R10

Ø20   10

A

30   50

25

A

24   26

34   52   24

Ø20

Ø10   Ø3   Ø3   Ø10

7

50

100

120

SECTION A-A

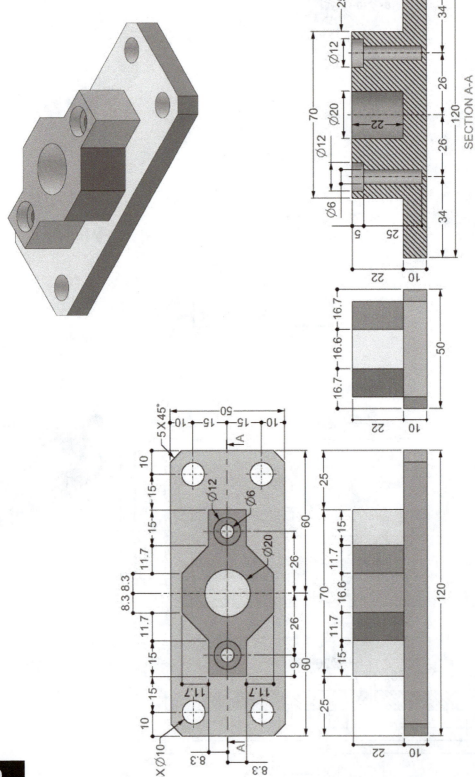

SECTION A-A

EX-39

70
R20
Ø20
40
45

R25
Ø20
45
20
30
10
A
A
45
65
10

20
2X R10
Ø40
Ø20
25
45

SECTION A-A

EX-40

Ø60
20
10
5
Ø50

Ø60
Ø50

5 10 5
30
Ø60
20

P-21

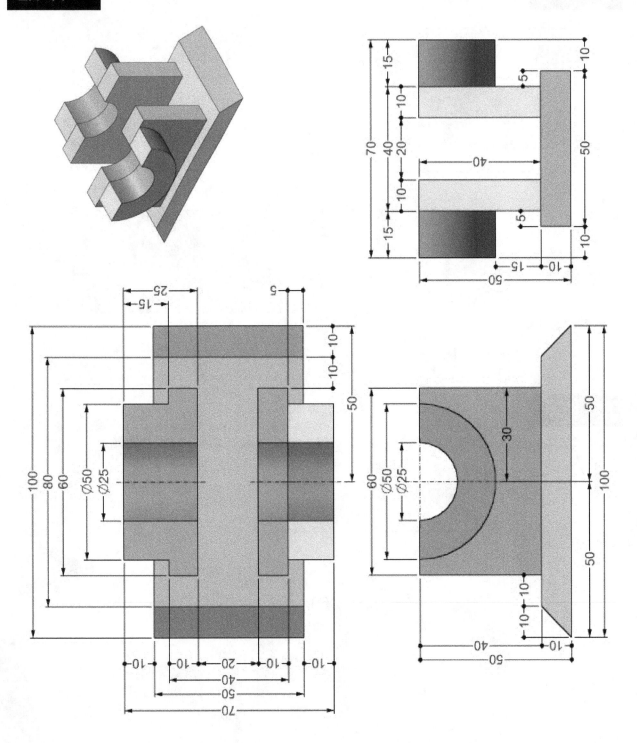

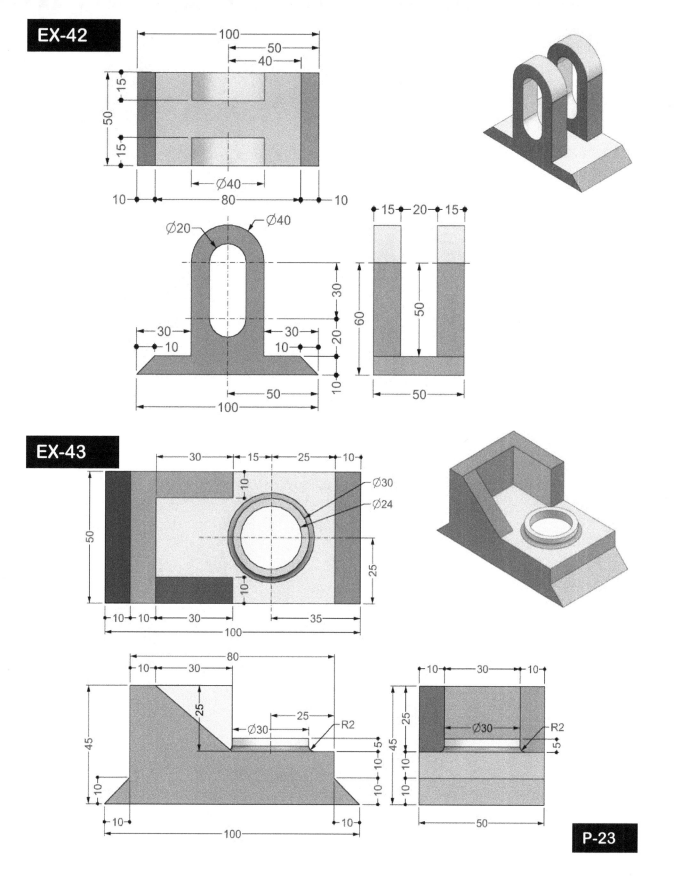

EX-42

EX-43

P-23

EX-44

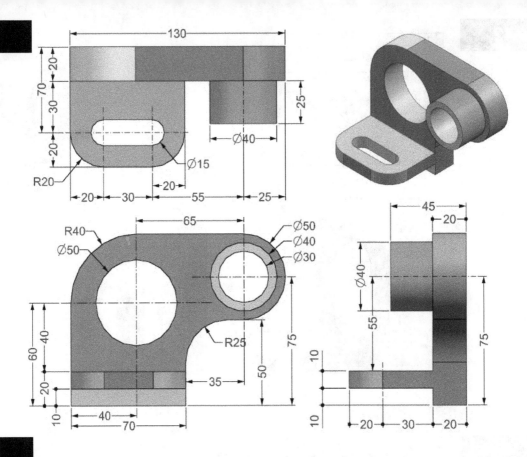

EX-45

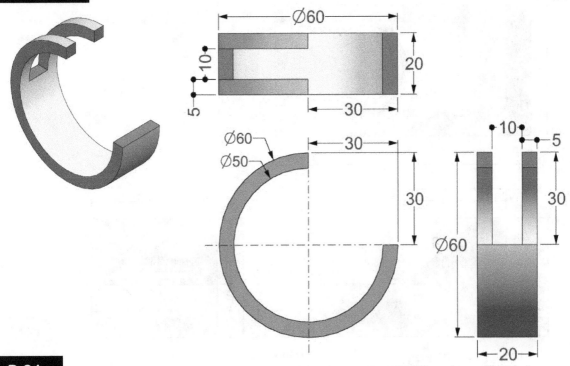

EX-46

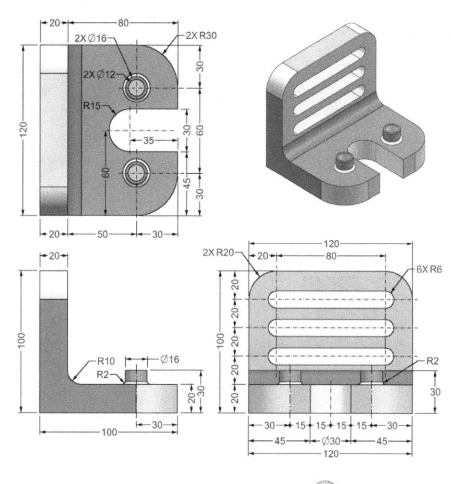

20 · 80 · 2X R30
2X Ø16
2X Ø12
2X R30
30
R15
120
60
30
35
30
60
45
30
20 · 50 · 30

20
100
R10
R2
Ø16
30
20
100 · 30

EX-47

2X R20 · 20 · 120 · 6X R6
80
20
20
20
100
20
20
20
20
R2
30
30 · 15 · 15 · 15 · 15 · 30
45 · Ø30 · 45
120

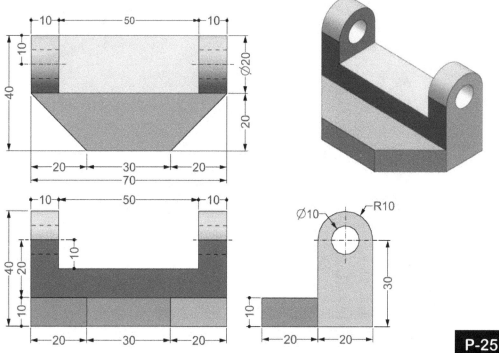

10 · 50 · 10
10
Ø20
40
20
20 · 30 · 20
70

10 · 50 · 10
40
20
10
10
20 · 30 · 20

Ø10
R10
30
10
20 · 20

EX-48

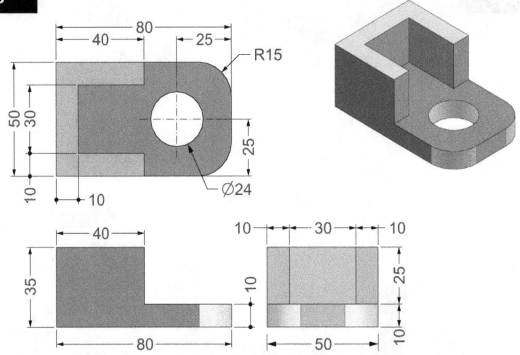

EX-49

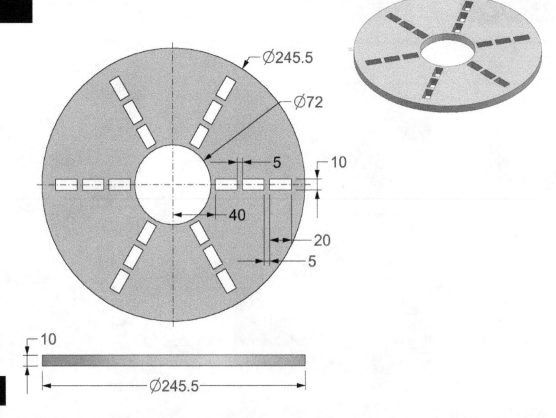

P-26

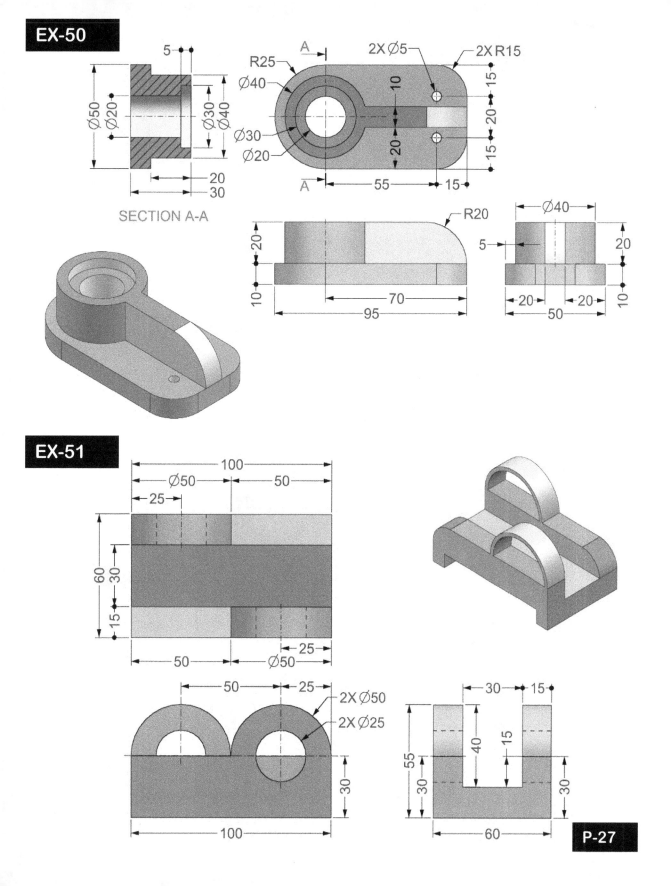

EX-50

SECTION A-A

EX-51

P-27

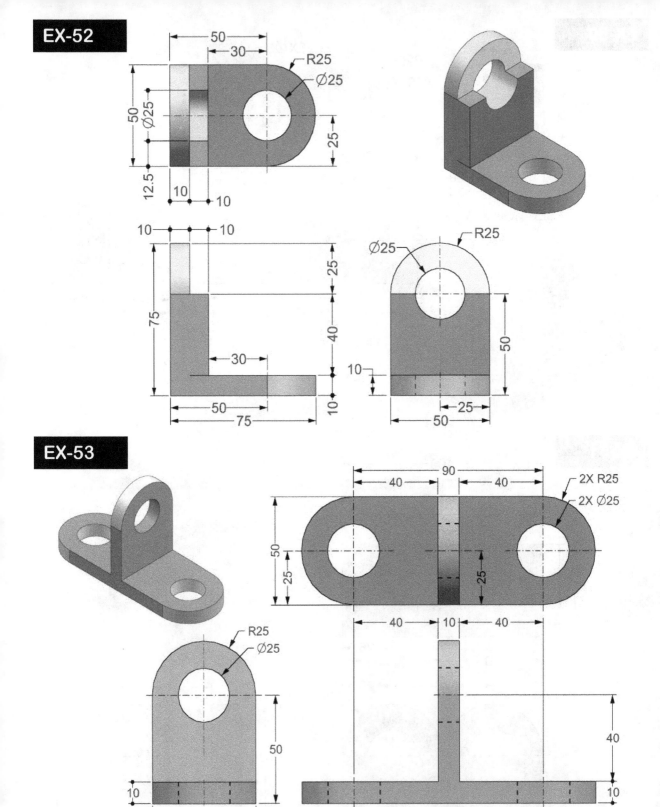

EX-52

EX-53

P-28

EX-54

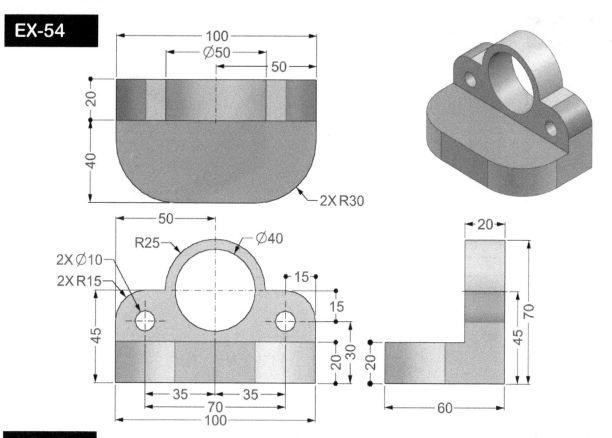

- 100
- Ø50
- 50
- 20
- 40
- 2X R30
- 50
- R25
- Ø40
- 2X Ø10
- 2X R15
- 15
- 15
- 45
- 20
- 30
- 35
- 35
- 70
- 100
- 20
- 70
- 45
- 20
- 60

EX-55

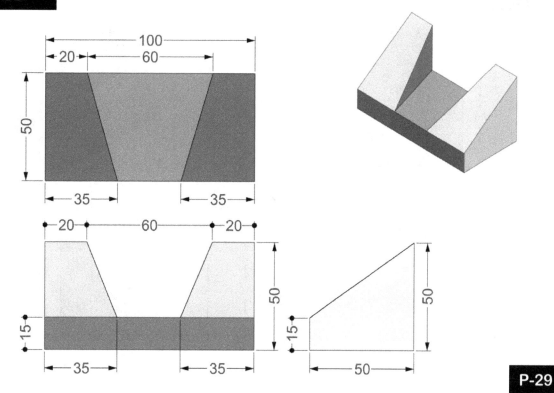

- 100
- 20
- 60
- 50
- 35
- 35
- 20
- 60
- 20
- 50
- 15
- 35
- 35
- 15
- 50
- 50

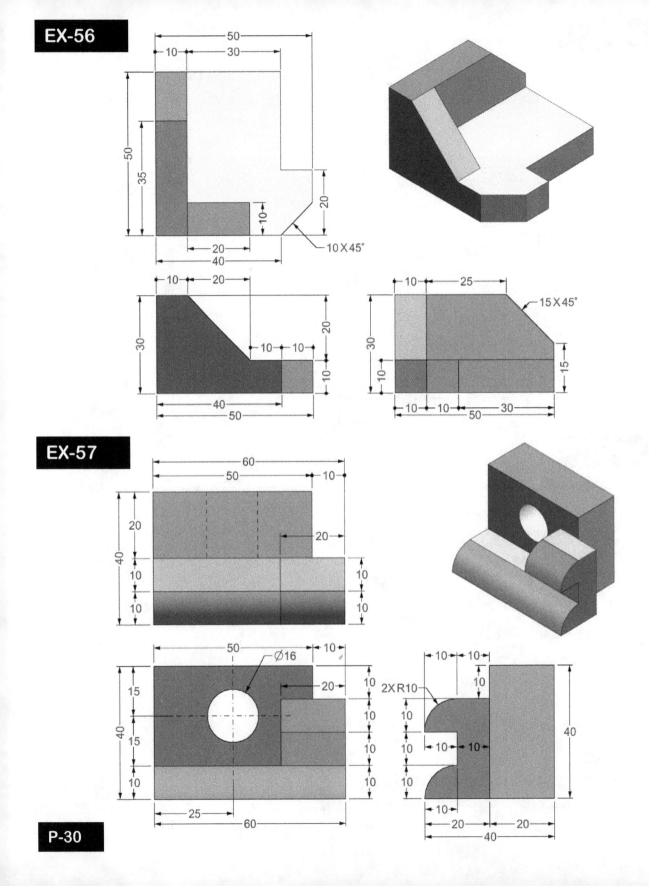

EX-56

10 X 45°
15 X 45°

EX-57

Ø16

2X R10

P-30

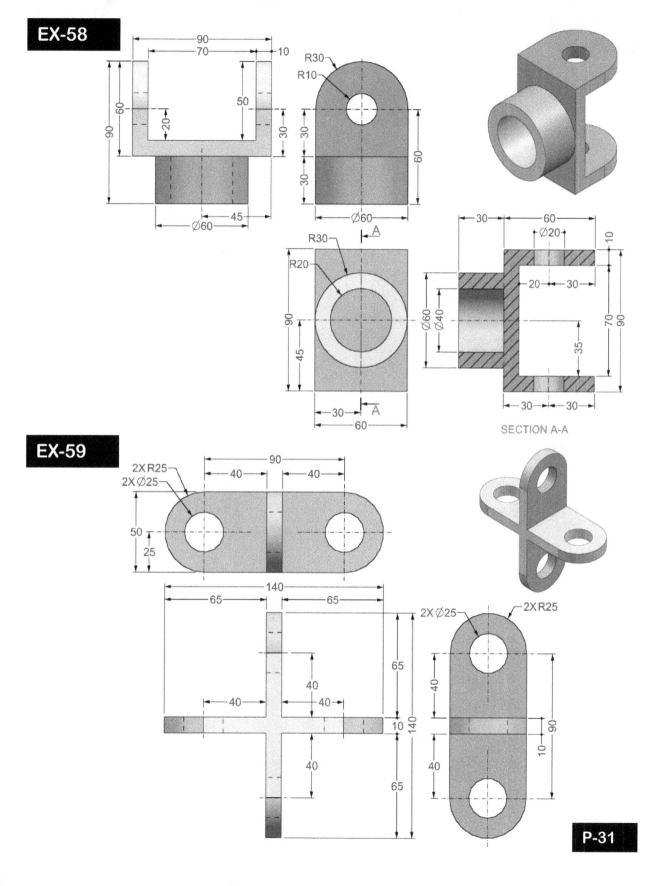

EX-58

90
70
10
R30
R10
60
50
90
20
30
30
60
45
Ø60
Ø60

R30
R20
A
90
45
30
60

30
60
Ø20
10
Ø60
Ø40
20
30
70
90
35
30
30

SECTION A-A

EX-59

2X R25
2X Ø25
90
40
40
50
25

140
65
65
65
40
40
40
40
10
140
40
65

2X Ø25
2X R25
40
40
10
90
40

P-31

Ø50
22.5 2X Ø10
15
25
60
43.9
10
15
25
50
45
95

Ø50
Ø40
R4 R10
10
R10
40
155
130
10
45 45
80
140
R10 R10
55
40
30
10 10
22.5 22.5
100

60
85.4
100
155
34.6
10 25
40
60

Ø120
20
R3
50
Ø50
10 10
R2
Ø50
Ø70

14 14
PCD Ø90
R60
Ø70
Ø30
Ø50
6X Ø10
66
14
132
14
A
A
66
66 66
132

132
Ø70
Ø50
Ø30
Ø10
10 10 10
R2
Ø50
Ø30
R3
Ø10
45 45
90
120
SECTION A-A
100
50
20

Ø120
6X Ø10
ON PCD 90
PCD Ø90
Ø30
66
132
14
14
66
14 14
66 66
132

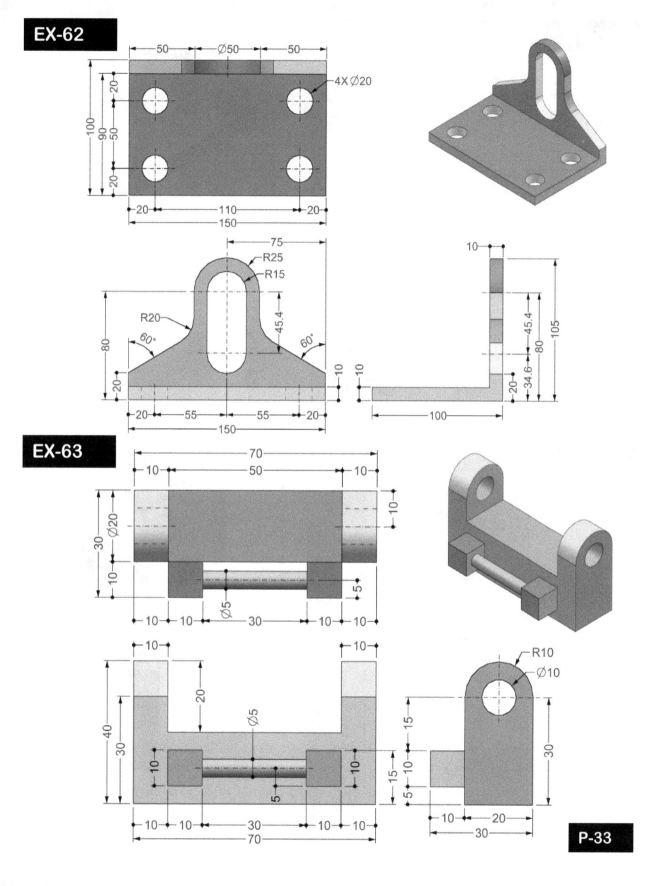

EX-62

EX-63

P-33

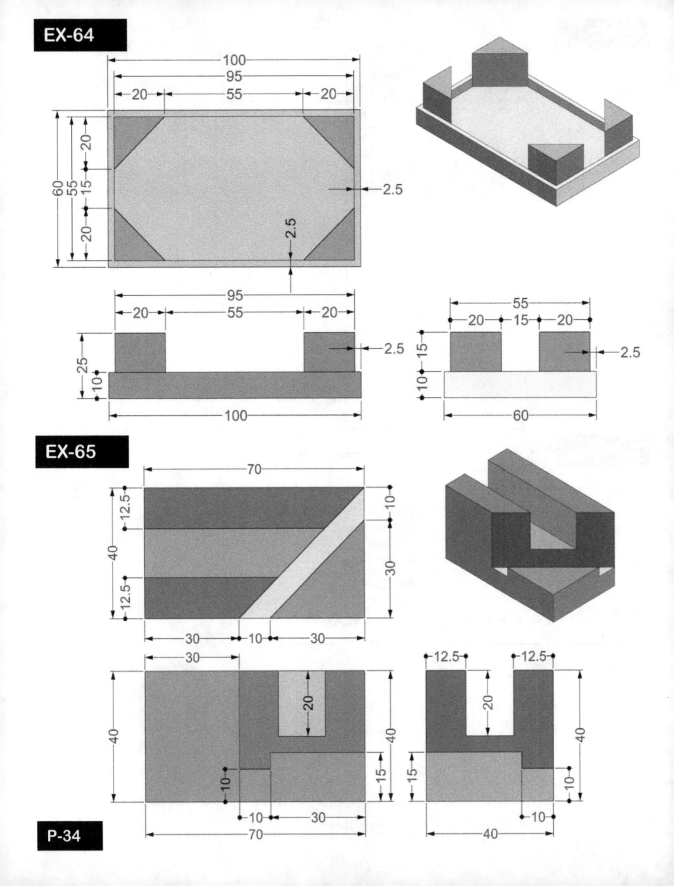

EX-64

100
95
20 | 55 | 20
60
55
20
15
20
2.5
2.5

95
20 | 55 | 20
25
10
100
2.5

55
20 | 15 | 20
15
10
2.5
60

EX-65

70
12.5
10
40
30
12.5
30 | 10 | 30

30
40
20
10
10 | 30
70

12.5 | 12.5
20
40
15
10
10
40

P-34

EX-66

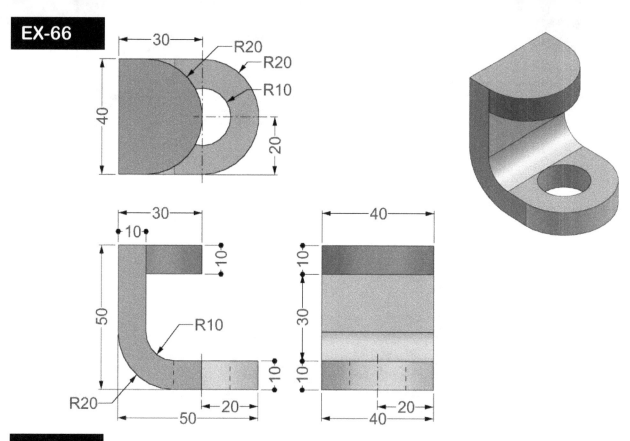

EX-67

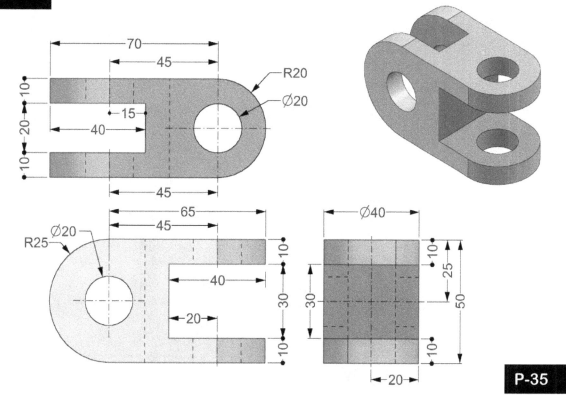

P-35

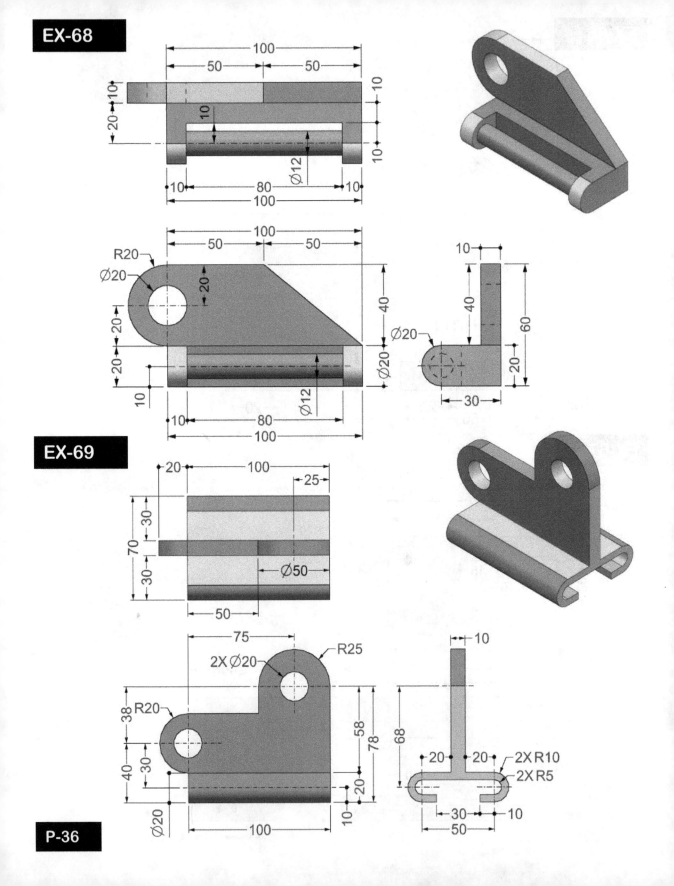

EX-68

EX-69

P-36

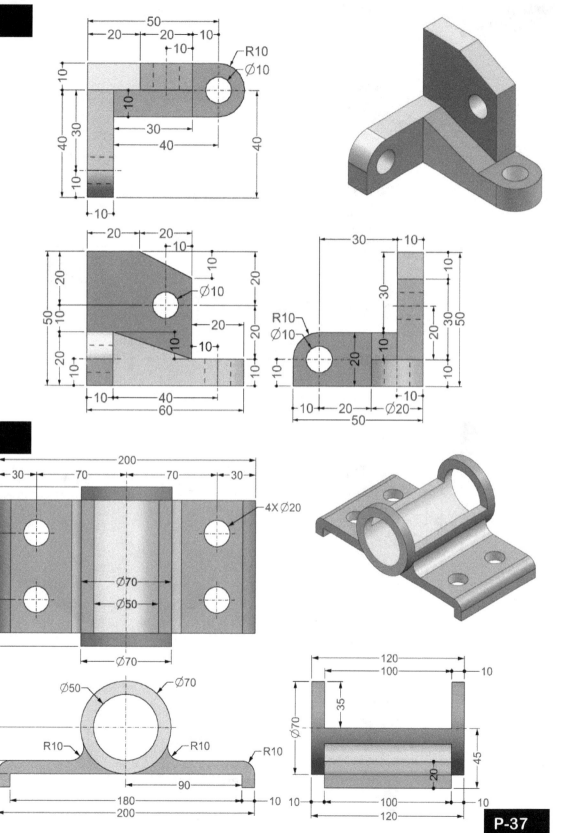

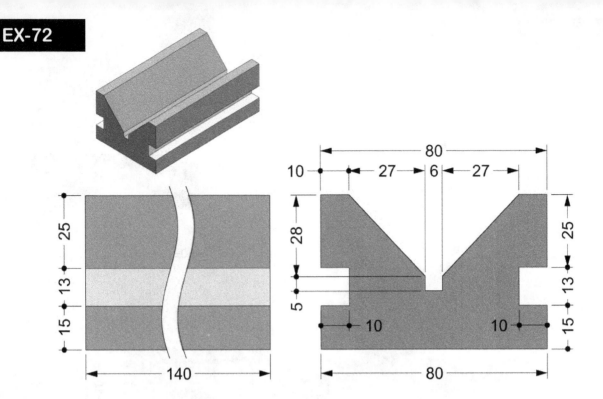

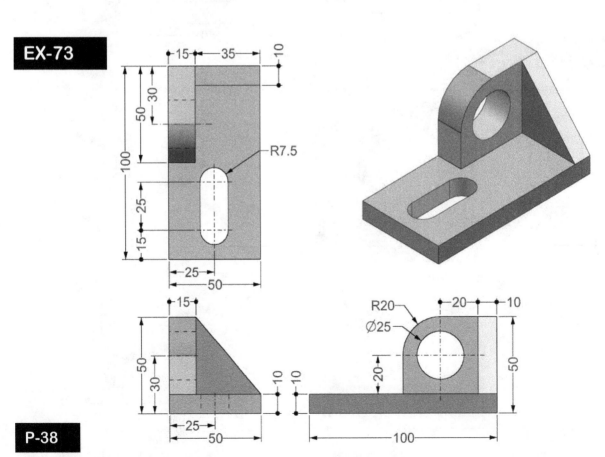

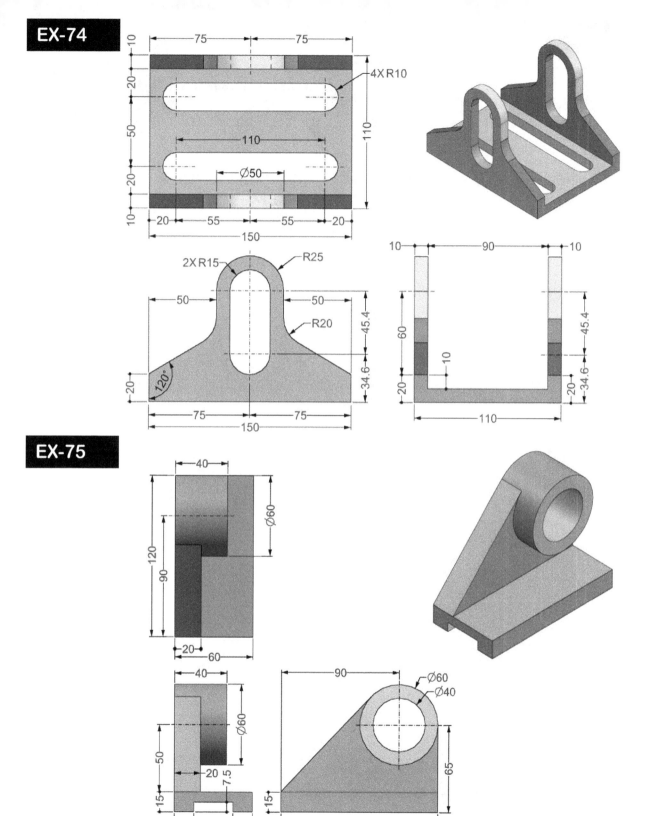

EX-74

4X R10
110
110
75 75
10
20
50
20
10
20 55 55 20
150

2X R15
R25
R20
50 50
45.4
34.6
120°
20
75 75
150

10 90 10
60
10
45.4
20 34.6
20
110

EX-75

40
Ø60
120
90
20
60

40
Ø60
50
20
7.5
15
15 30
60

90
Ø60
Ø40
65
15
120

P-39

EX-76

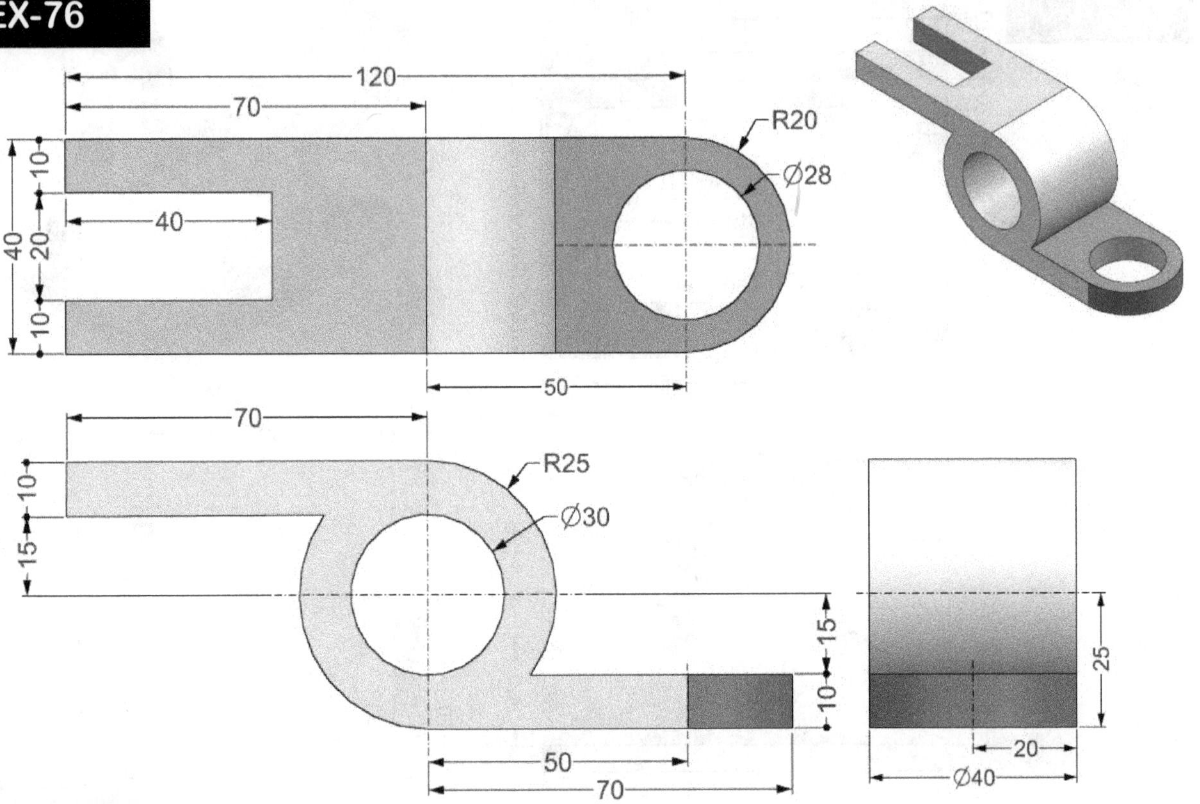

EX-77

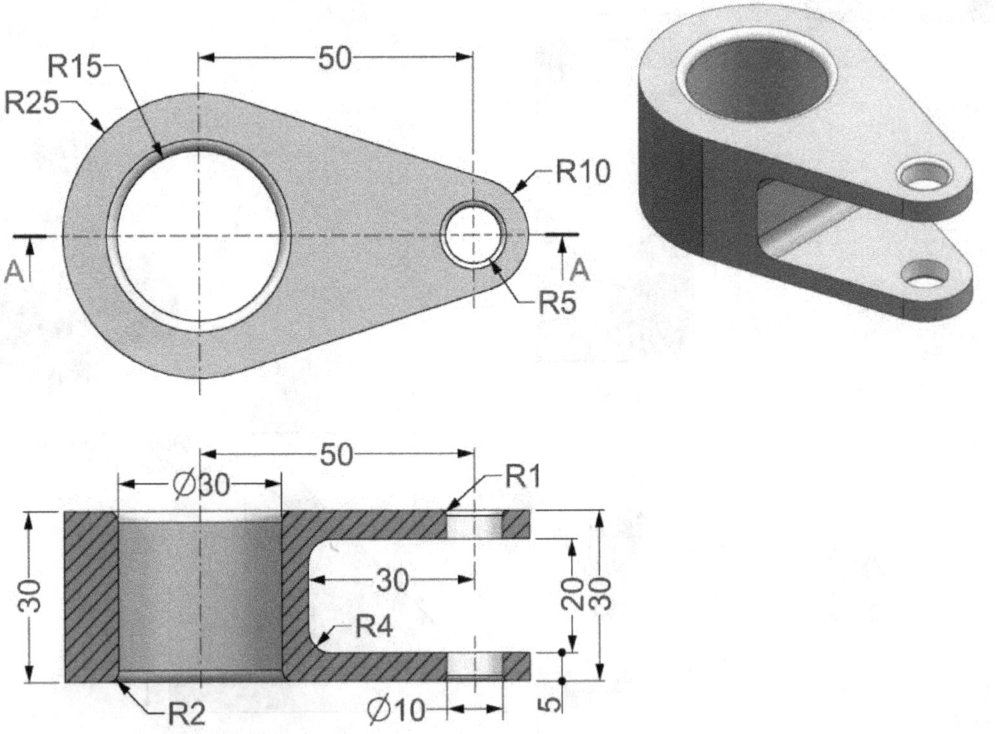

R15
R25
R10
R5

A — A

SECTION A-A

Ø30
50
R1
30
30
20
R4
R2
Ø10
5

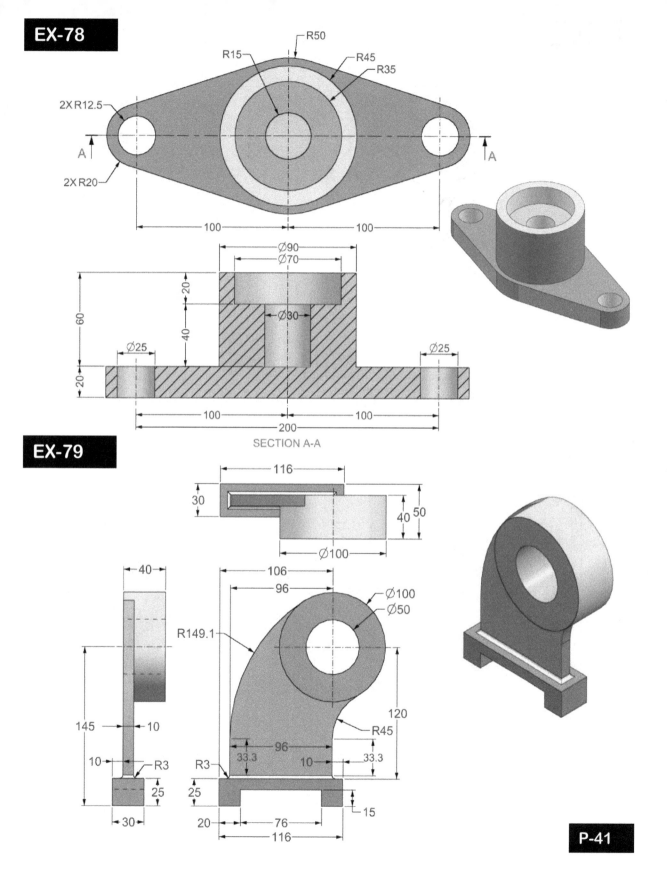

EX-78

R50
R15
R45
R35
2X R12.5
2X R20
100
100

Ø90
Ø70
20
60
40
Ø30
Ø25
Ø25
20
100
100
200
SECTION A-A

EX-79

116
30
40 50
Ø100

106
96
Ø100
Ø50
R149.1
40
120
145
10
R45
96
33.3
10
33.3
10
R3
R3
25
25
30
15
20
76
116

P-41

EX-80

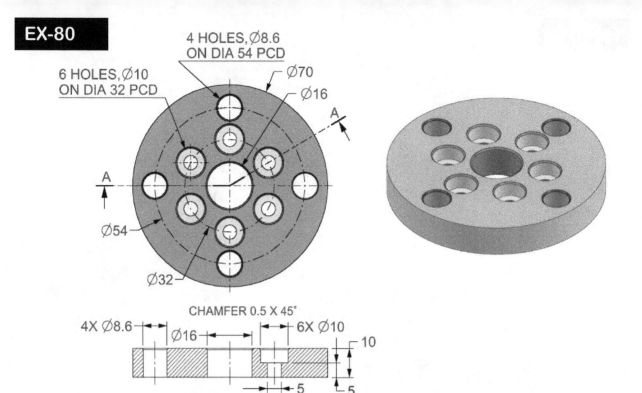

6 HOLES, Ø10
ON DIA 32 PCD

4 HOLES, Ø8.6
ON DIA 54 PCD

Ø70

Ø16

A

A

Ø54

Ø32

CHAMFER 0.5 X 45°

4X Ø8.6

Ø16

6X Ø10

10

5

5

SECTION A-A
(SCALE 1:1)

EX-81

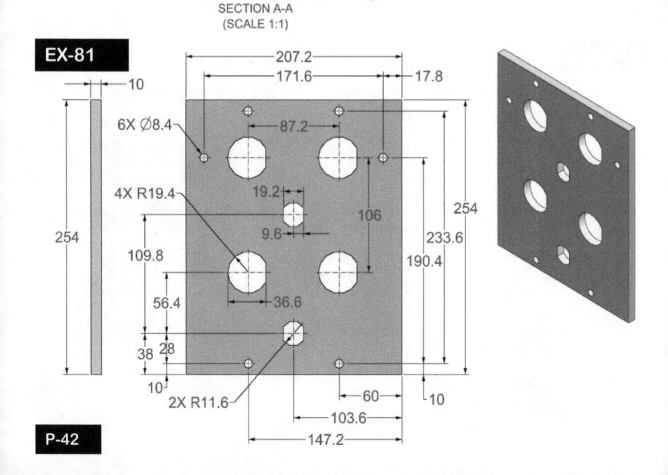

207.2

171.6

17.8

10

6X Ø8.4

87.2

4X R19.4

19.2

106

254

9.6

233.6

190.4

254

109.8

56.4

36.6

38

28

2X R11.6

10

60

10

103.6

147.2

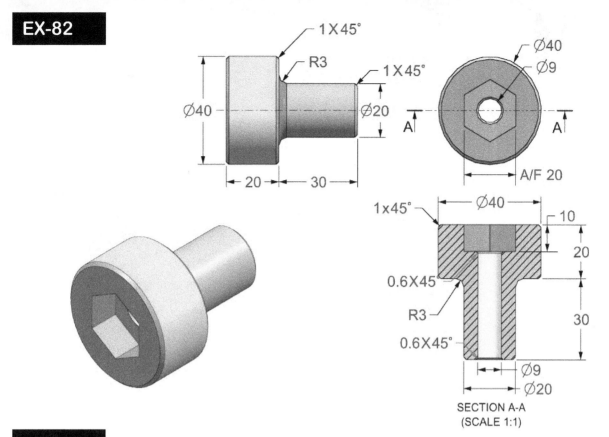

1 X 45°
R3
1 X 45°
Ø40
Ø20
Ø40
Ø9
A
A
A/F 20
20
30

1x45°
Ø40
10
20
0.6X45°
R3
0.6X45°
30
Ø9
Ø20

SECTION A-A
(SCALE 1:1)

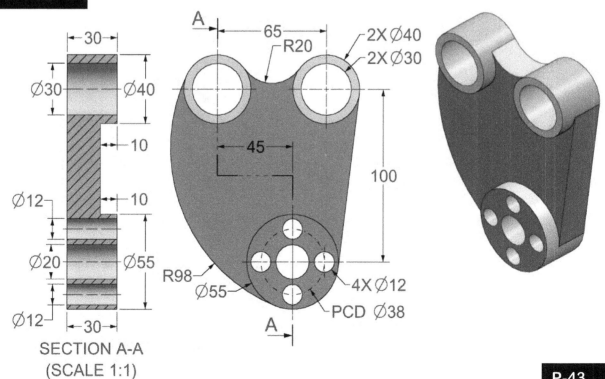

30
Ø30
Ø40
10
10
Ø12
Ø20
Ø55
Ø12
30

SECTION A-A
(SCALE 1:1)

A
65
R20
2X Ø40
2X Ø30
45
100
R98
Ø55
4X Ø12
PCD Ø38
A

EX-84

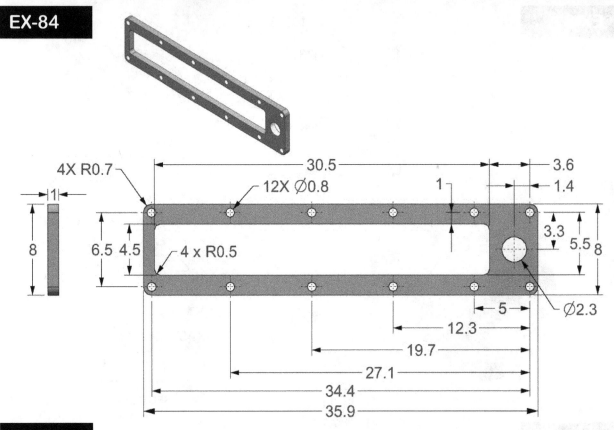

4X R0.7

12X ⌀0.8

4 x R0.5

30.5   3.6   1.4   1   3.3   5.5   8

6.5   4.5   1   8

5   ⌀2.3

12.3

19.7

27.1

34.4

35.9

EX-85

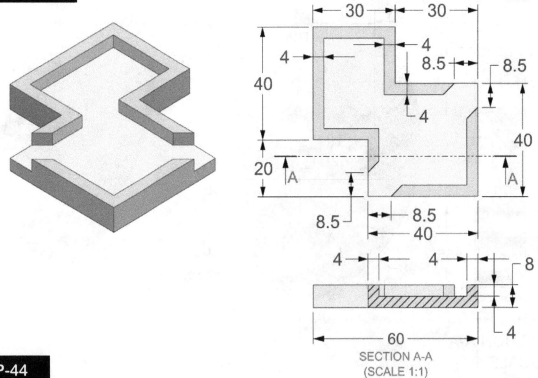

30   30

4   4   8.5   8.5

40   4

20   A   40

A

8.5   8.5

8.5   40

4   4   8

60   4

SECTION A-A
(SCALE 1:1)

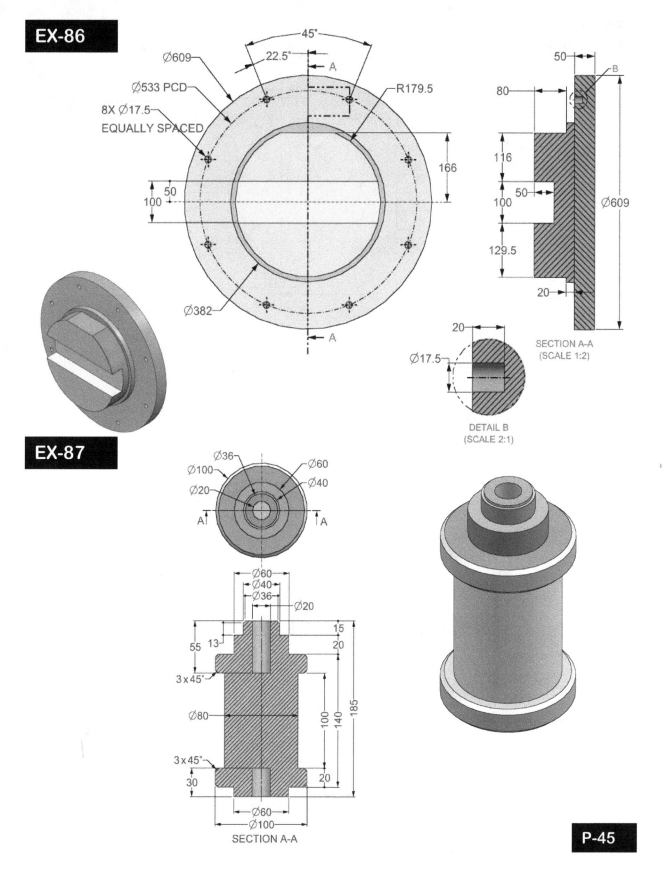

EX-86

∅609
∅533 PCD
8X ∅17.5
EQUALLY SPACED
45°
22.5°
A
R179.5
166
50
100
∅382
A

50
80
B
116
100
50
129.5
20
∅609

SECTION A-A
(SCALE 1:2)

20
∅17.5

DETAIL B
(SCALE 2:1)

EX-87

∅36
∅100
∅20
∅60
∅40
A   A

∅60
∅40
∅36
∅20
15
13
20
55
3 x 45°
∅80
100
140
185
20
3 x 45°
30
∅60
∅100

SECTION A-A

P-45

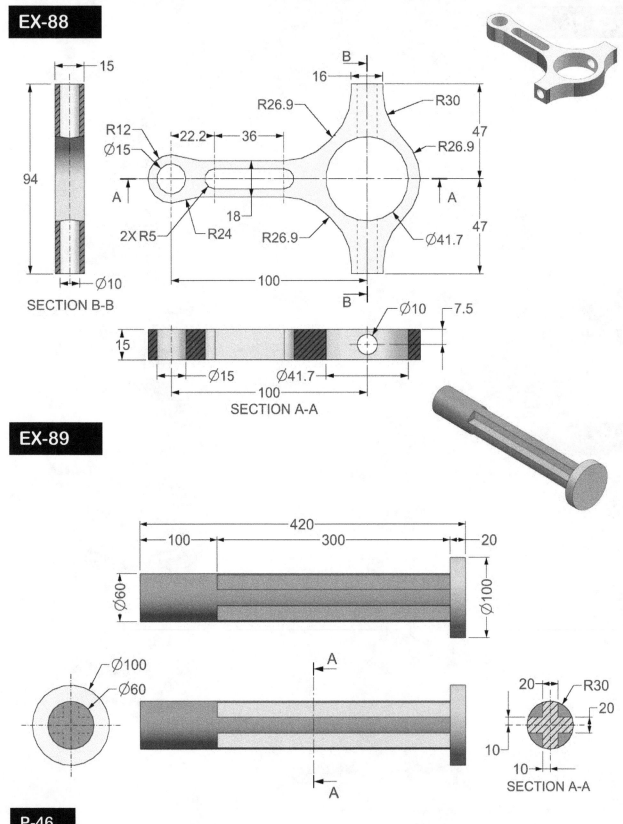

EX-88

15

94

Ø10

SECTION B-B

R12
Ø15
22.2
36
B
16
R26.9
R30
47
R26.9
47
2X R5
R24
18
R26.9
Ø41.7
100
B

15
Ø10
7.5
Ø15
Ø41.7
100
SECTION A-A

EX-89

420
100
300
20
Ø60
Ø100

Ø100
Ø60

A
A

20
R30
20
10
10
SECTION A-A

P-46

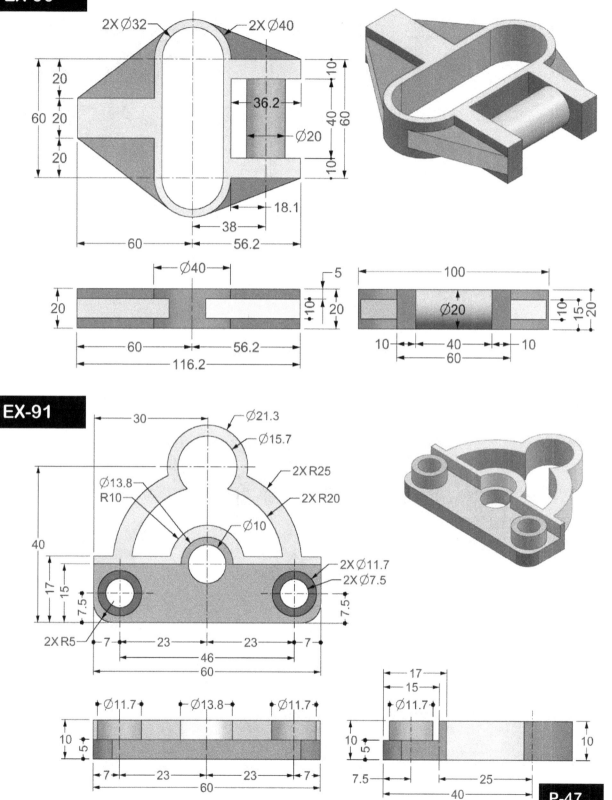

EX-90

2X Ø32
2X Ø40
20
60 20
20
10
40
60
10
36.2
Ø20
18.1
38
60
56.2

Ø40
20
60
56.2
116.2

5
10 20

100
Ø20
10 15 20
10
40
10
60

EX-91

30
Ø21.3
Ø15.7
2X R25
Ø13.8
R10
2X R20
Ø10
40
17
15
7.5
2X Ø11.7
2X Ø7.5
7.5
2X R5
7
23
23
7
46
60

Ø11.7
Ø13.8
Ø11.7
10
5
7
23
23
7
60

17
15
Ø11.7
10
5
7.5
25
40

10

P-47

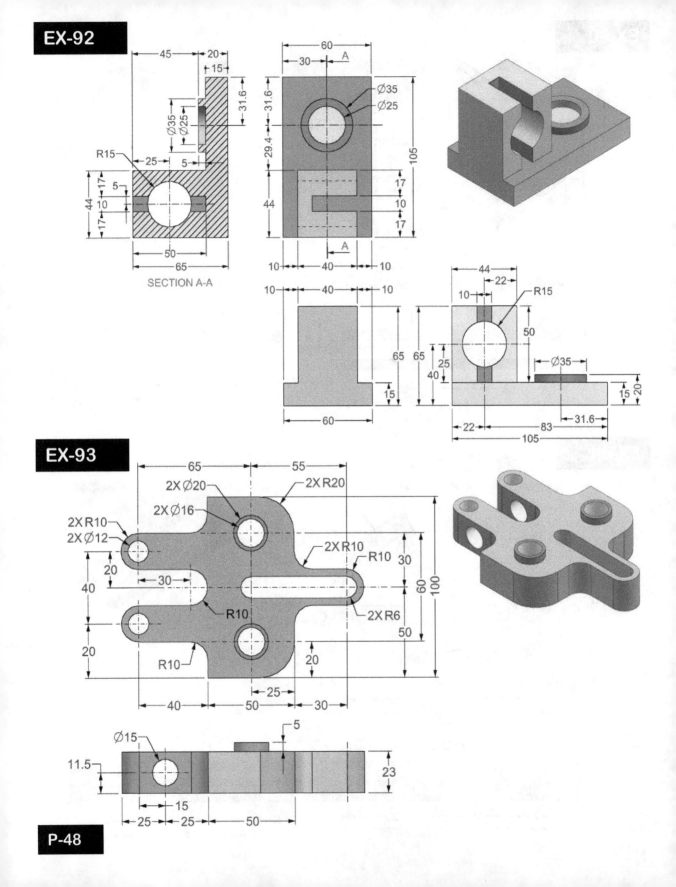

EX-92

R15

Ø35
Ø25

45
20
15
31.6

25
5

44
17
5
10
17

50
65

SECTION A-A

60
30
A

Ø35
Ø25

31.6
29.4
44

17
10
17
105

10
40
10

A

10
40
10

65
15

60

44
22
R15

10
50

25
40

Ø35

65
65

15
20

22
83
31.6
105

EX-93

65
55

2X Ø20
2X R20
2X Ø16
2X R10
2X Ø12

2X R10
R10
30

20
40
30
60
100

R10

2X R6

20
R10

50

20

25
40
50
30

5

Ø15
11.5

23

15
25
25
50

P-48

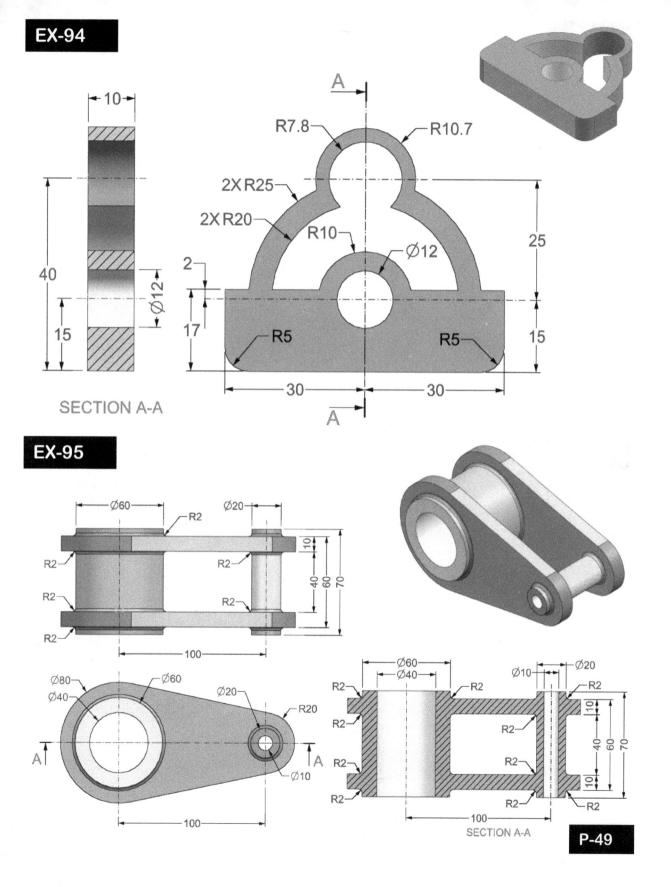

EX-94

10

R7.8   R10.7

2X R25

2X R20   R10   Ø12

40   Ø12

2

17

15   R5   R5

25

15

30   30

A

A

SECTION A-A

EX-95

Ø60   R2   Ø20

R2   10   R2

R2   40   60   70

R2   R2

R2

100

Ø80   Ø60   Ø20

Ø40   R20

A   A

Ø10

100

Ø60   R2   Ø10   Ø20

Ø40   R2   R2

R2   10

R2   R2   40   60   70

R2   R2

R2   R2   R2   10   R2

100   R2

SECTION A-A

P-49

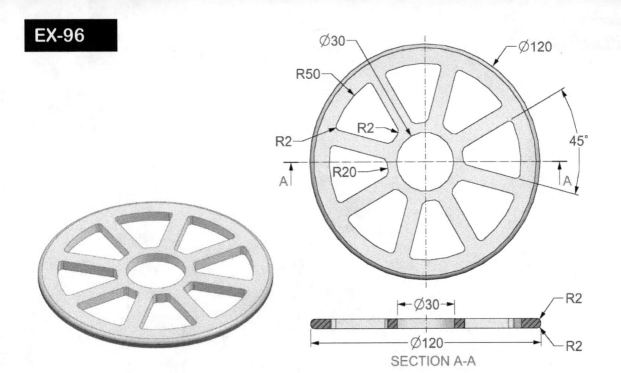

Ø30
Ø120
R50
R2
R2
R2
R20
45°
A
A

Ø30
Ø120
R2
R2
SECTION A-A

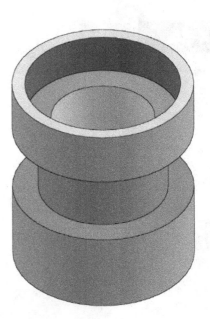

Ø70
Ø60
Ø40
A
A

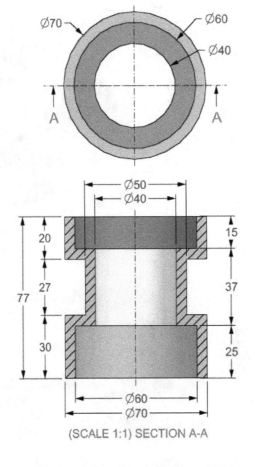

Ø50
Ø40
20
15
27
37
77
30
25
Ø60
Ø70
(SCALE 1:1) SECTION A-A

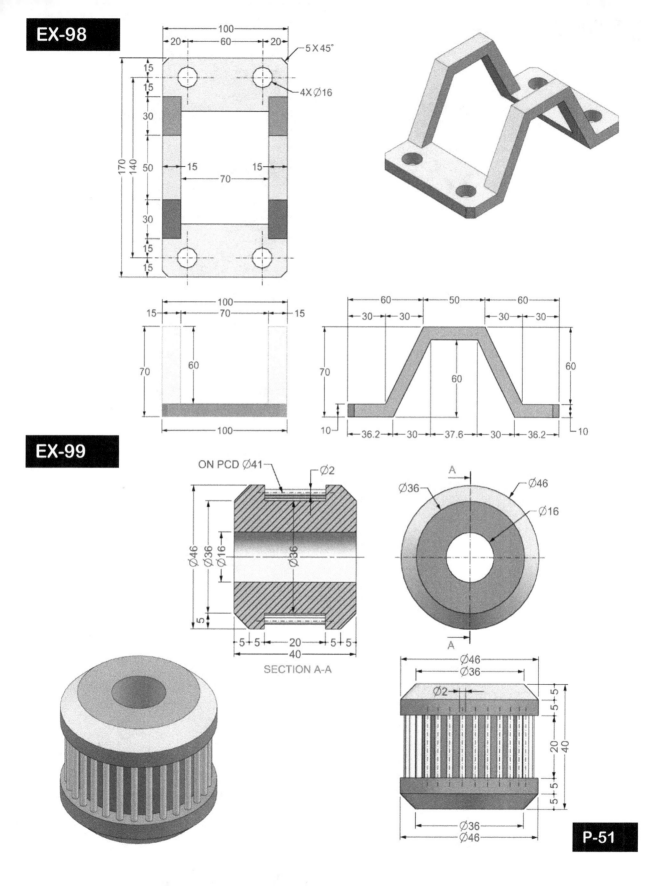

EX-98

EX-99

ON PCD Ø41

SECTION A-A

P-51

EX-100

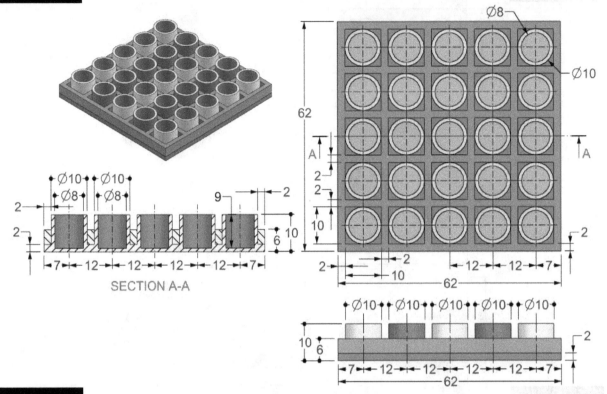

SECTION A-A

EX-101

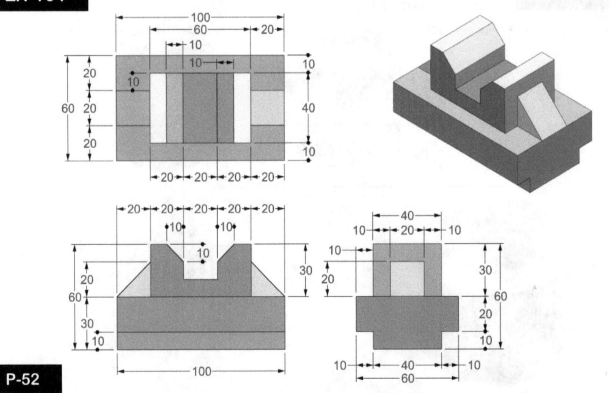

P-52

EX-102

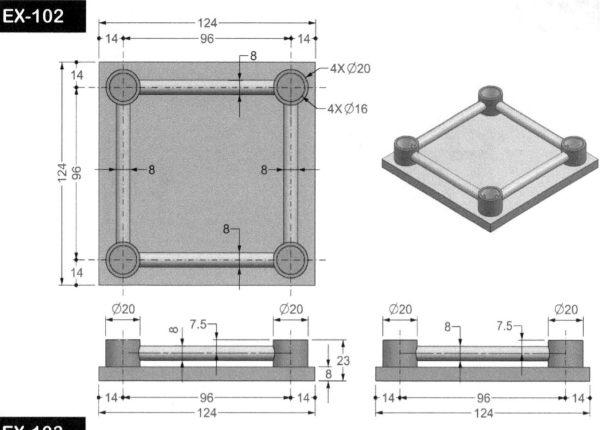

EX-103

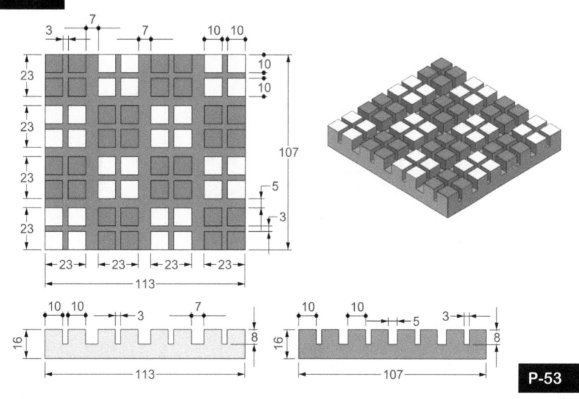

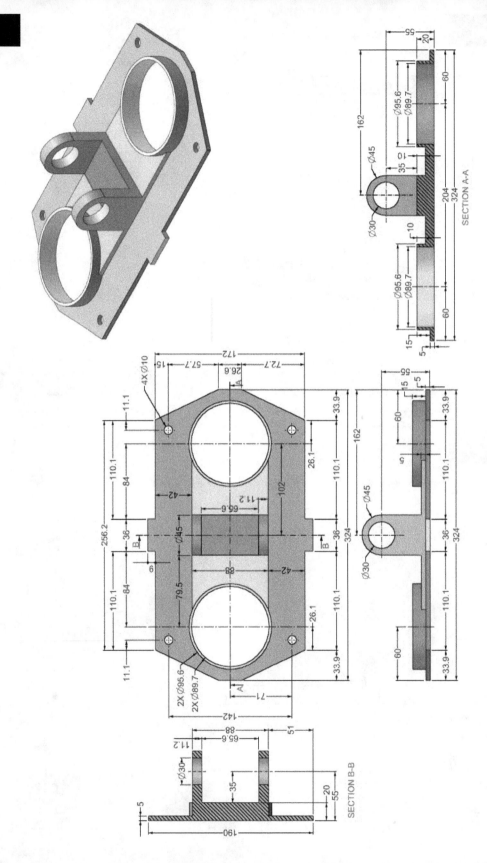

SECTION A-A

SECTION B-B

EX-105

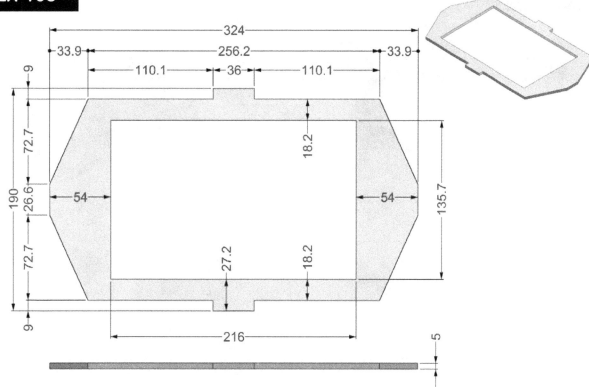

EX-106

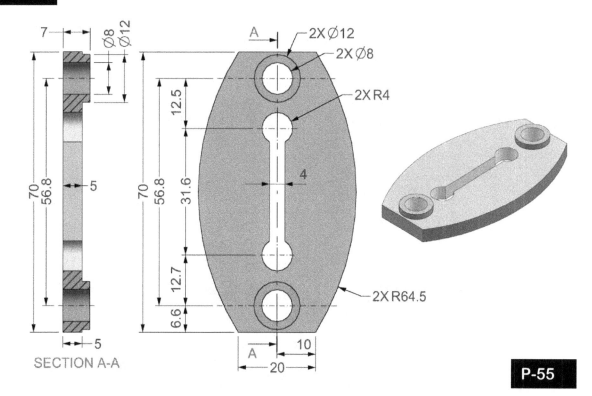

SECTION A-A

EX-107

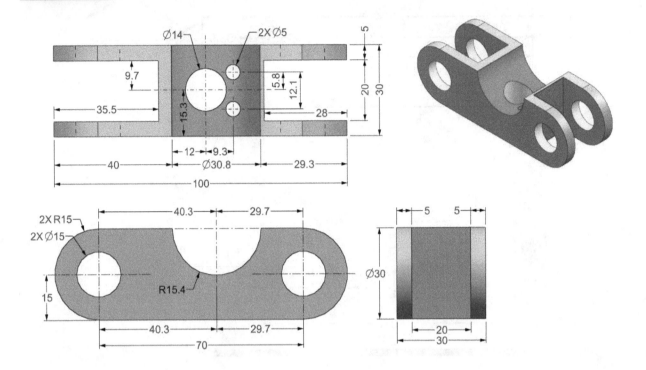

EX-108

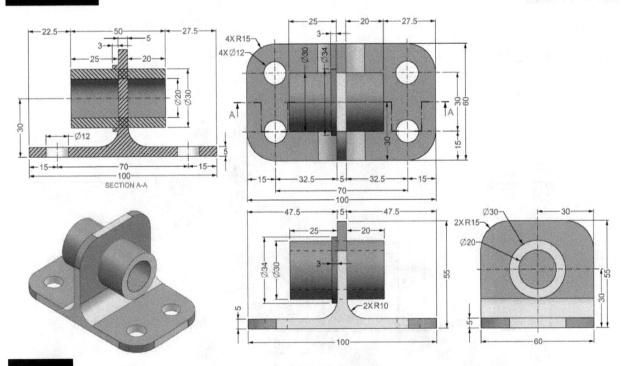

SECTION A-A

P-56

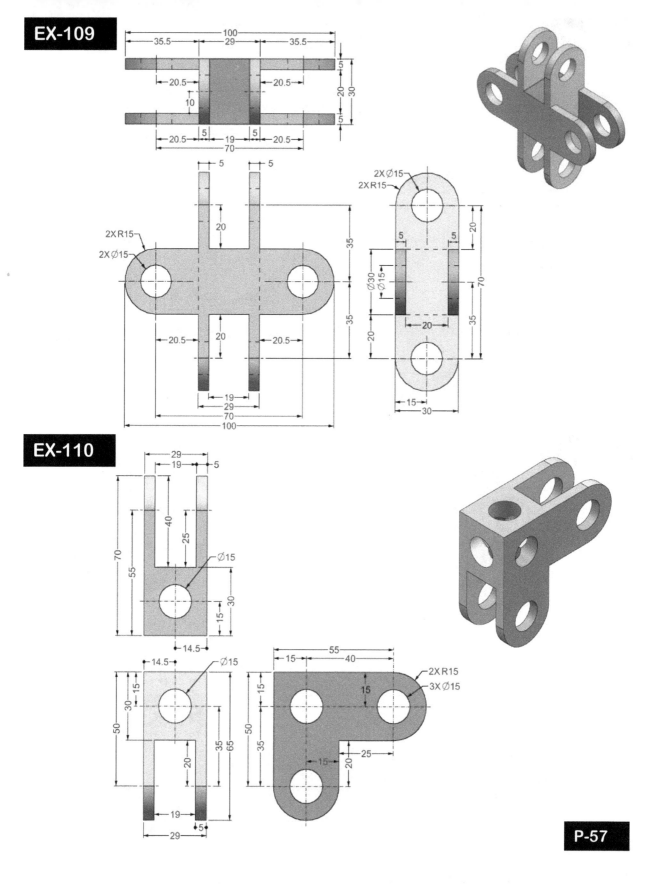

EX-109

EX-110

P-57

EX-111

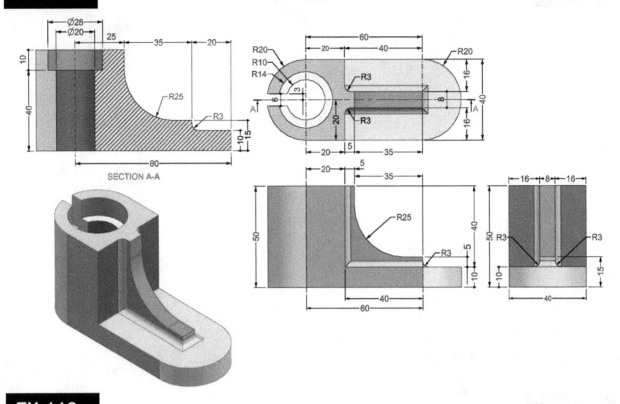

SECTION A-A

EX-112

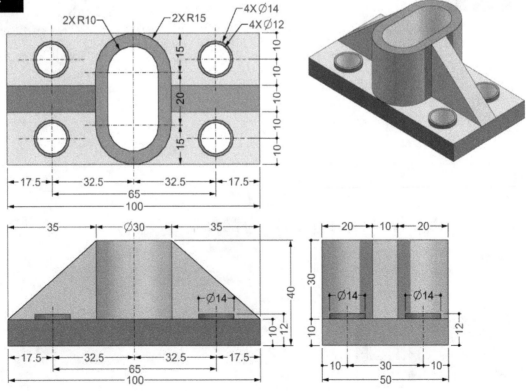

P-58

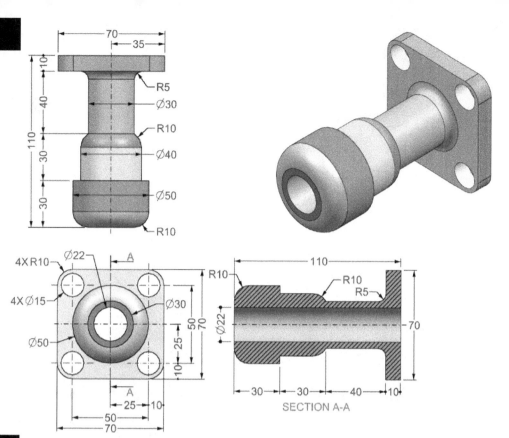

70
35
10
40
110
30
30
R5
Ø30
R10
Ø40
Ø50
R10

4X R10
Ø22
A
4X Ø15
Ø30
Ø50
50
70
25
10
A
25
10
50
70

R10
110
R10
R5
Ø22
70
30
30
40
10

SECTION A-A

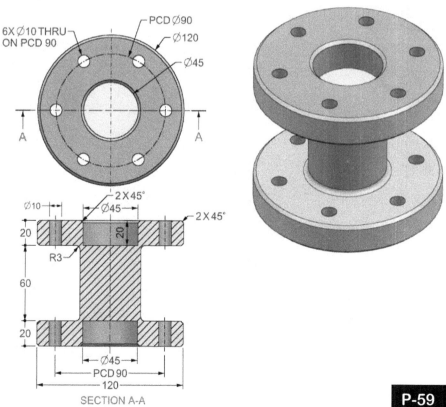

6X Ø10 THRU
ON PCD 90
PCD Ø90
Ø120
Ø45
A
A

Ø10
2 X 45°
Ø45
2 X 45°
20
20
R3
60
20
Ø45
PCD 90
120

SECTION A-A

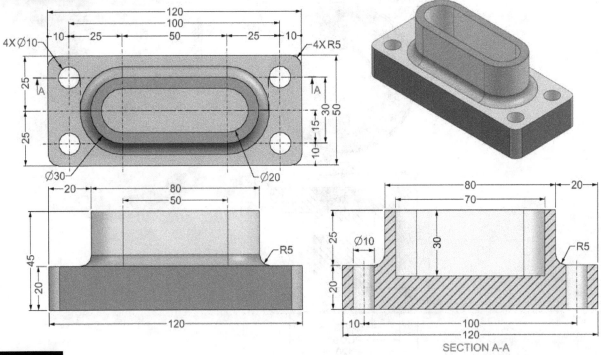

Ø120
6X Ø10
6X Ø8
PCD Ø90
Ø68
A | A
Ø45

Ø120
Ø68
Ø10
R2
10
10
20
120
60
20
10
PCD 90

Ø120
PCD 90
Ø68
Ø45
Ø10
2 X 45°
40
20
60
R3
R3
Ø8
Ø55
Ø50
20
Ø45
Ø8
SECTION A-A

120
100
10 25 50 25 10
4X Ø10
4X R5
25
A | A
30 50
25
15
10
Ø30
Ø20

20
80
50
45
20
R5
120

80 20
70
25
Ø10
30
R5
20
10 100
120
SECTION A-A

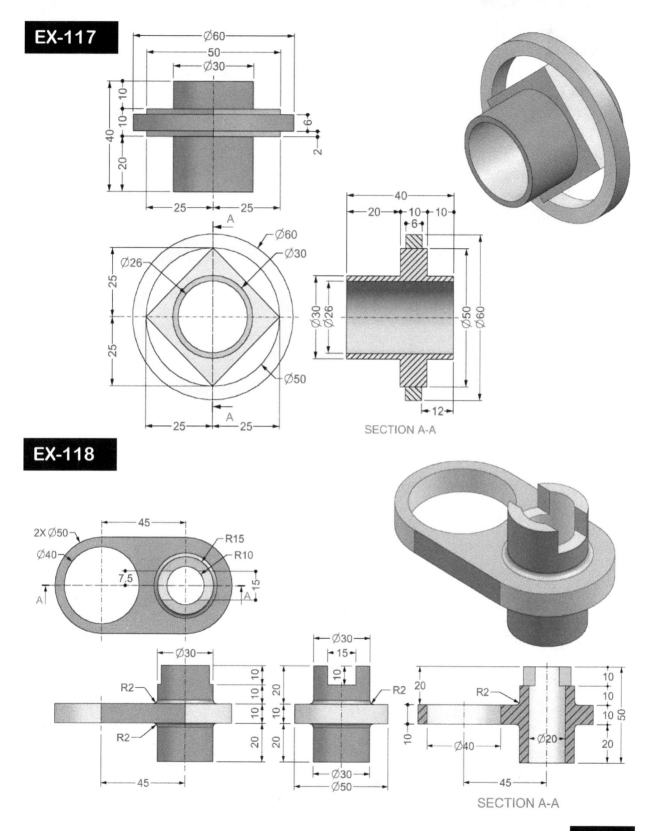

EX-117

Ø60
50
Ø30
10
10
6
40
2
20
25 | 25

A

Ø60
Ø30
Ø26
25
25
Ø50
25 | 25
A

40
20 | 10 | 10
6
Ø30
Ø26
Ø50
Ø60
12

SECTION A-A

EX-118

2X Ø50
Ø40
45
R15
R10
7.5
15
A | A

Ø30
R2
10 | 10
10 | 10
20
10 | 10
R2
20
45

Ø30
15
10
20 | 10 | 20
R2
Ø30
Ø50

Ø30
20
R2
10
Ø40
Ø20
45
10 | 10 | 10 | 20
50

SECTION A-A

P-61

EX-119

Ø190
Ø55

Ø140
70
2X R20
2X R25
25
50
Ø55
Ø75
Ø100
Ø180
Ø190

SECTION A-A

A

R25
25
50
Ø75
Ø190

A

Ø75
Ø190
Ø55
Ø180
Ø100

EX-120

Ø50
Ø60
10
15
20
20
20
40
20
20
15
45
100

R15
A
Ø50
Ø70
Ø70
Ø40
A
Ø20
Ø30
Ø60
100
100

Ø50
Ø30
Ø60
Ø40
10
20
15
20
20
40
90
20
Ø20
15
20
45
100
100

SECTION A-A

P-62

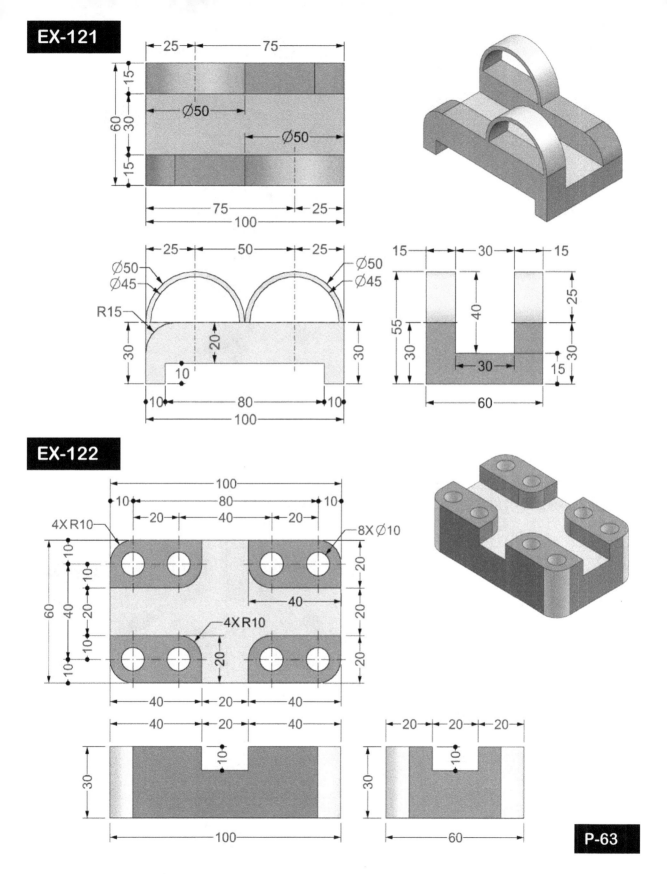

EX-121

EX-122

P-63

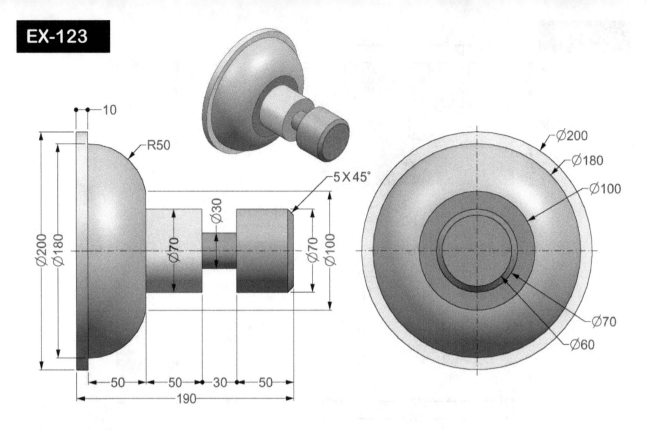

10
R50
5×45°
Ø30
Ø70
Ø70
Ø100
Ø200
Ø180
50 50 30 50
190

Ø200
Ø180
Ø100
Ø70
Ø60

EX-124

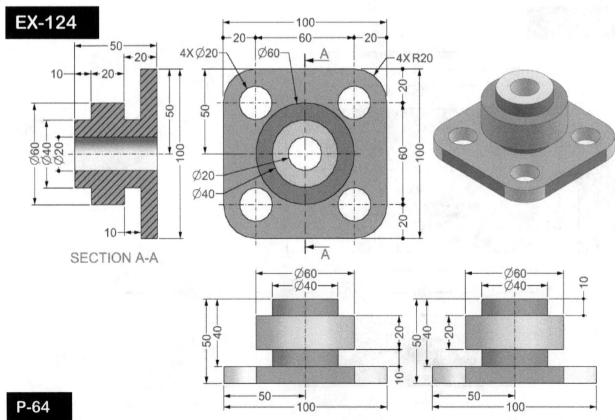

50
20
10 20
50
100
Ø60
Ø40
Ø20
10

SECTION A-A

100
20 60 20
4X Ø20
Ø60
A
4X R20
20
50
60
100
Ø20
Ø40
20
A

Ø60
Ø40
50
40
20
50
100

Ø60
Ø40
10
50
40
20
50
100

EX-125

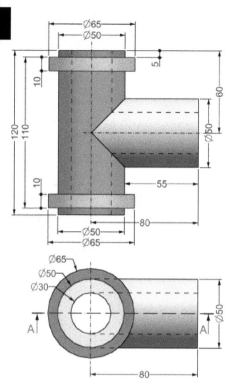

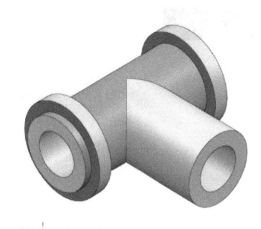

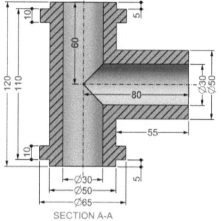

SECTION A-A

EX-126

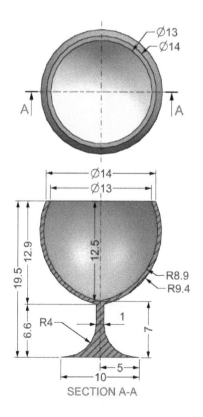

SECTION A-A

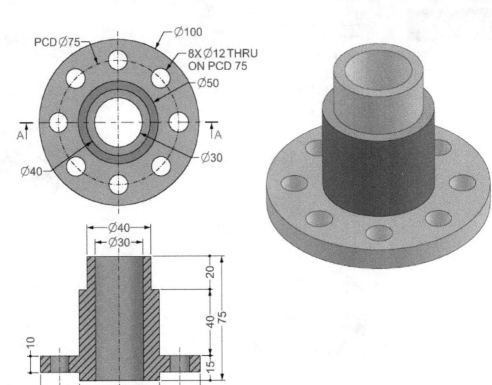

PCD Ø75
Ø100
8X Ø12 THRU
ON PCD 75
Ø50
Ø30
Ø40
A
A

Ø40
Ø30
20
40
75
10
15
Ø50
75
Ø100
SECTION A-A

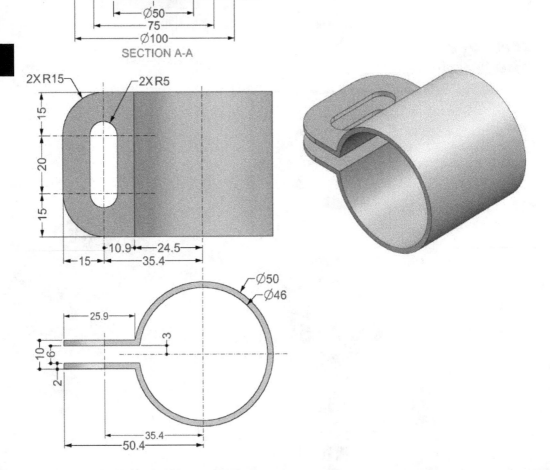

2X R15
2X R5
15
20
15
10.9
24.5
15
35.4

Ø50
Ø46
25.9
3
10
6
2
35.4
50.4

EX-129

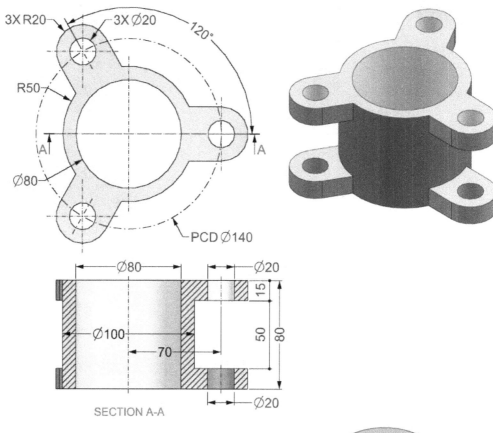

3X R20 3X ⌀20 120°

R50

A

⌀80

PCD ⌀140

⌀80 ⌀20

15

50 80

⌀100

70

⌀20

SECTION A-A

EX-130

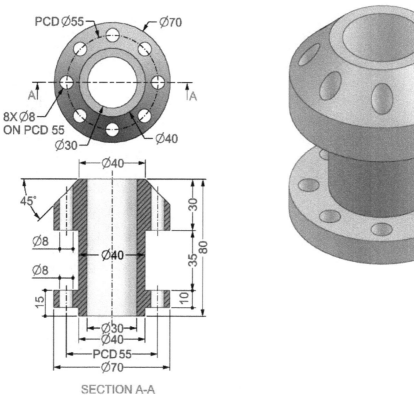

PCD ⌀55 ⌀70

A

8X ⌀8
ON PCD 55

⌀30 ⌀40

⌀40

45°

30

⌀8

⌀40 80

⌀8

35

15

10

⌀30
⌀40

PCD 55

⌀70

SECTION A-A

EX-131

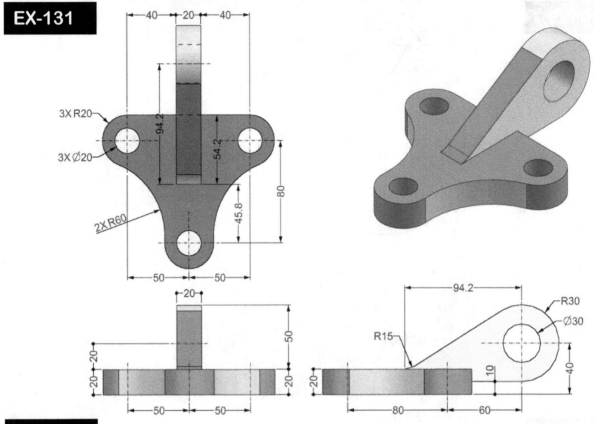

EX-132

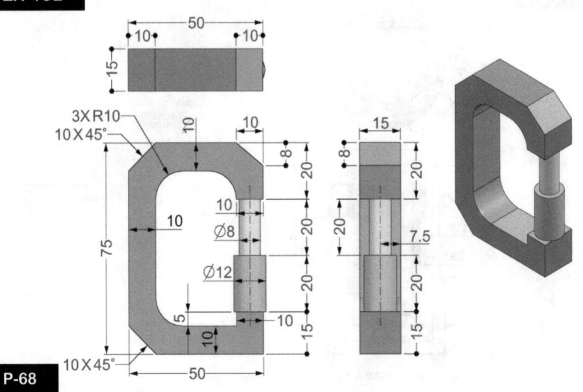

EX-133

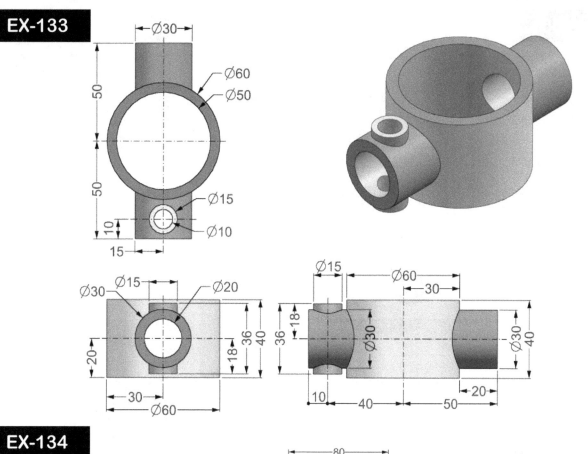

EX-134

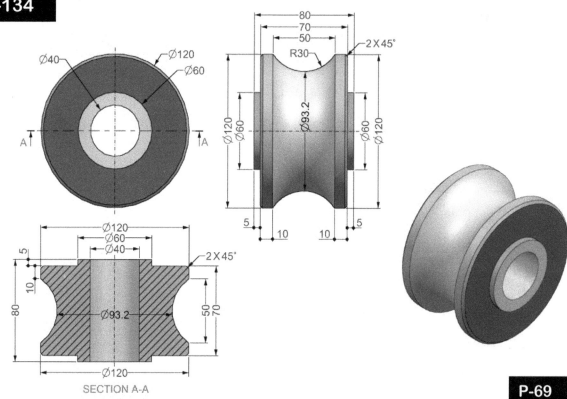

SECTION A-A

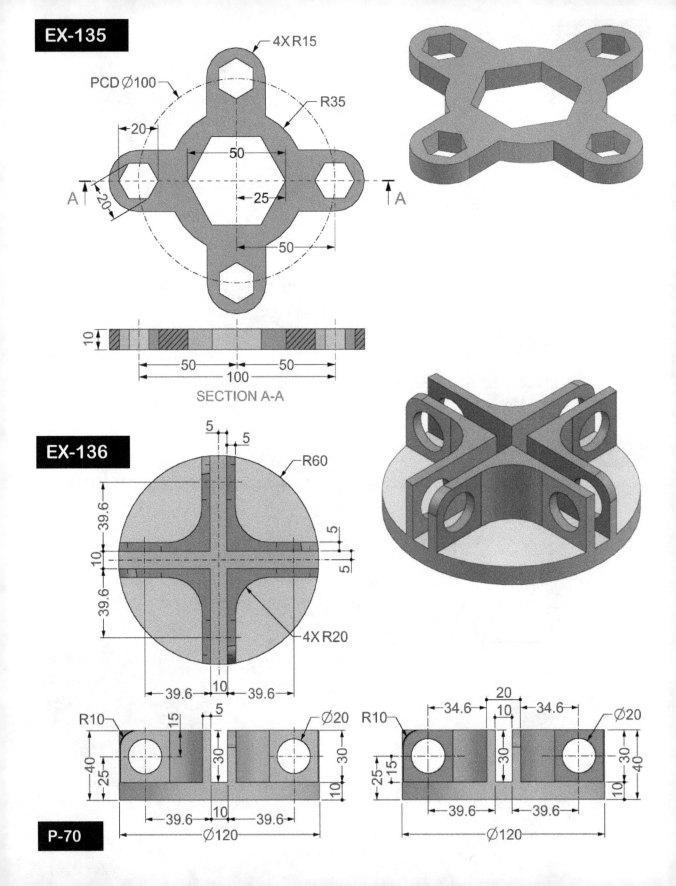

EX-135

4X R15

PCD Ø100

R35

20

50

25

20

A — A

50

SECTION A-A

10

50

50

100

EX-136

5

5

R60

39.6

10

5

5

39.6

4X R20

39.6

10

39.6

R10

5

15

30

Ø20

40

25

30

10

39.6

10

39.6

Ø120

R10

20

34.6

10

34.6

Ø20

25

15

30

30

40

10

39.6

39.6

Ø120

P-70

EX-137

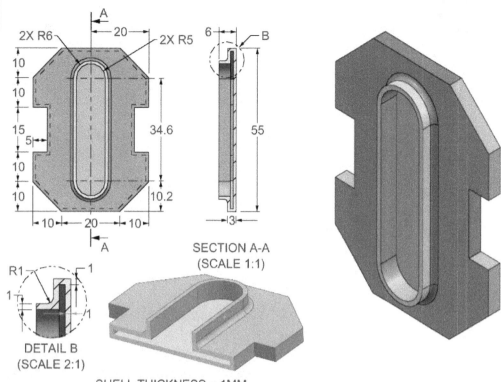

2X R6
2X R5
20
10
10
15
5
10
10
34.6
10.2
10
20
10
A
A
6
B
55
3

SECTION A-A
(SCALE 1:1)

R1
1
1
1

DETAIL B
(SCALE 2:1)

SHELL THICKNESS = 1MM
ALL INSIDE WALL THICKNESS

EX-138

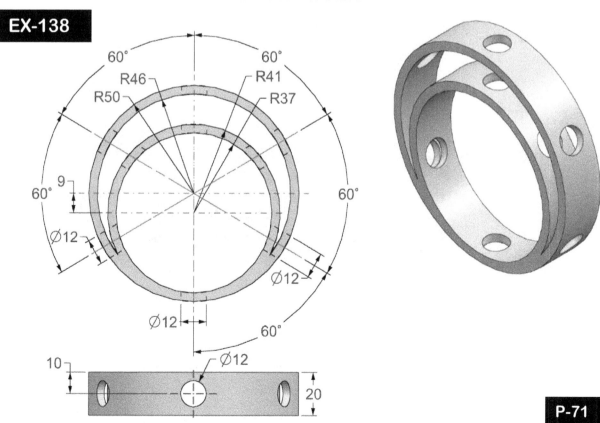

60°
60°
R46
R41
R50
R37
60°
9
60°
Ø12
Ø12
Ø12
60°
10
Ø12
20

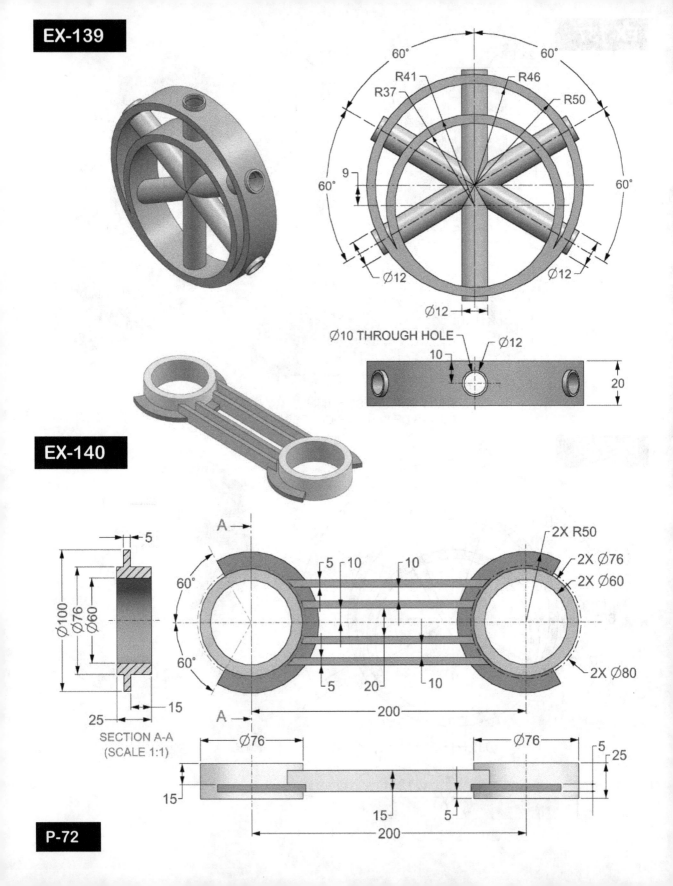

EX-139

60° 60°
R41 R46
R37
R50

60° 9 60°

60° 60°

Ø12 Ø12

Ø12

Ø10 THROUGH HOLE Ø12

10
20

EX-140

5

Ø100 Ø76 Ø60

15

25

SECTION A-A
(SCALE 1:1)

A

60°

60°

A

5 10 10

5

20 10

200

2X R50
2X Ø76
2X Ø60

2X Ø80

Ø76 Ø76
5
25

15

15 5

200

P-72

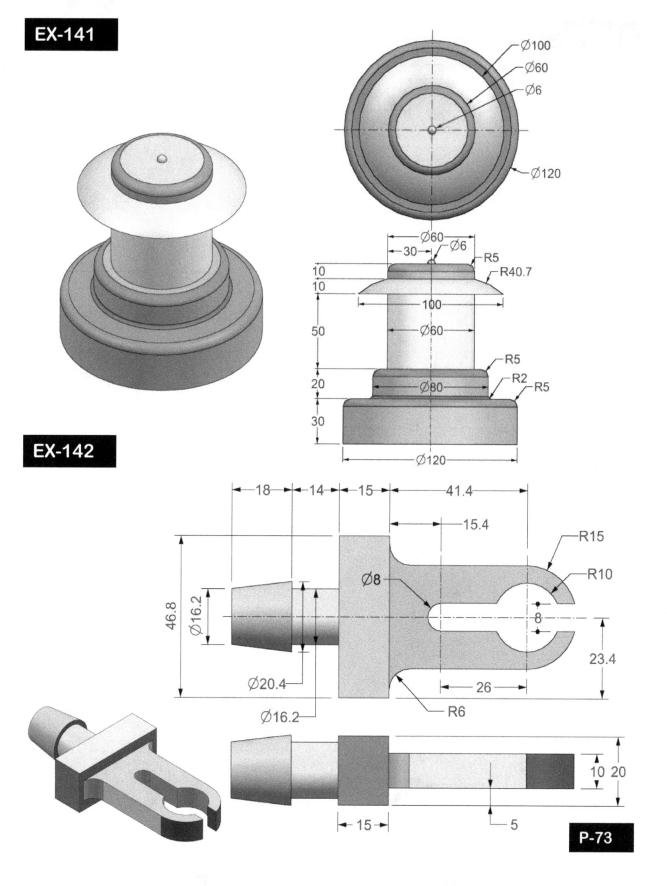

EX-141

EX-142

Ø100
Ø60
Ø6
Ø120

Ø60
30
Ø6
R5
R40.7
10
10
100
50
Ø60
R5
20
R2 R5
Ø80
30
Ø120

18
14
15
41.4
15.4
R15
R10
Ø8
46.8
Ø16.2
8
Ø20.4
23.4
Ø16.2
26
R6

10 20
15
5

P-73

EX-143

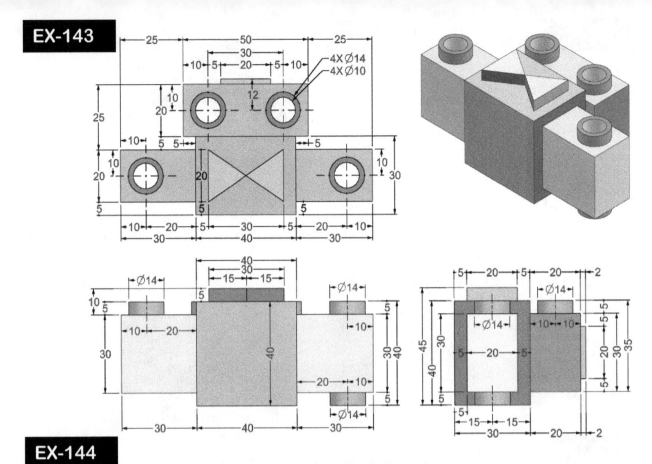

EX-144

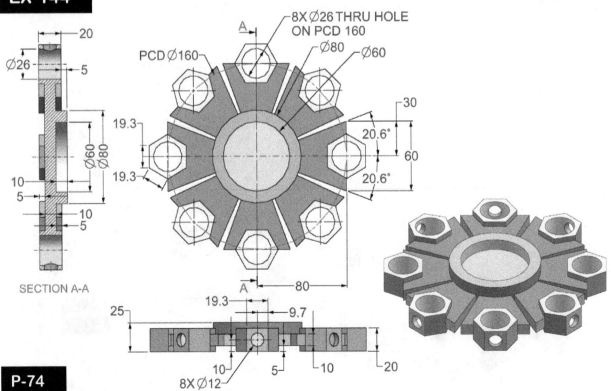

SECTION A-A

8X Ø26 THRU HOLE ON PCD 160

PCD Ø160

Ø80   Ø60

8X Ø12

P-74

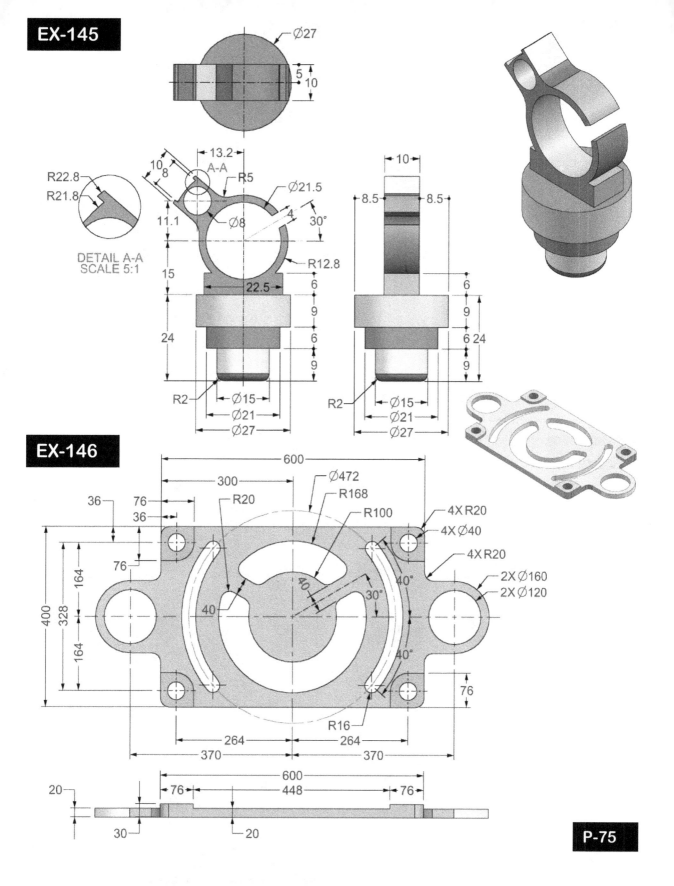

EX-145

Ø27
5
10

13.2
A-A
R5
Ø21.5
10
8
R22.8
R21.8
11.1
Ø8
4
30°
DETAIL A-A
SCALE 5:1
15
R12.8
22.5
6
9
24
6
9
R2
Ø15
Ø21
Ø27

10
8.5   8.5
6
9
6 24
9
R2
Ø15
Ø21
Ø27

EX-146

600
300
Ø472
R168
36
76
R20
R100
4X R20
36
4X Ø40
76
4X R20
164
76
2X Ø160
400
328
40
40°
2X Ø120
164
40
30°
40°
40°
76
R16
264   264
370   370

20
600
76   448   76
30   20

P-75

Ø40
Ø20
120°
120°
10
60

R10
Ø40
200
79.6
Ø20
15
R15
60

2X Ø100
2X Ø80
Ø50
R45
R40
Ø30
51.6
100
100

A
A

Ø90
Ø50
10
10
40
15
100
100

Ø90
Ø80
Ø50
Ø30
Ø80
Ø80
10
15
40
10
15
100
100

SECTION A-A

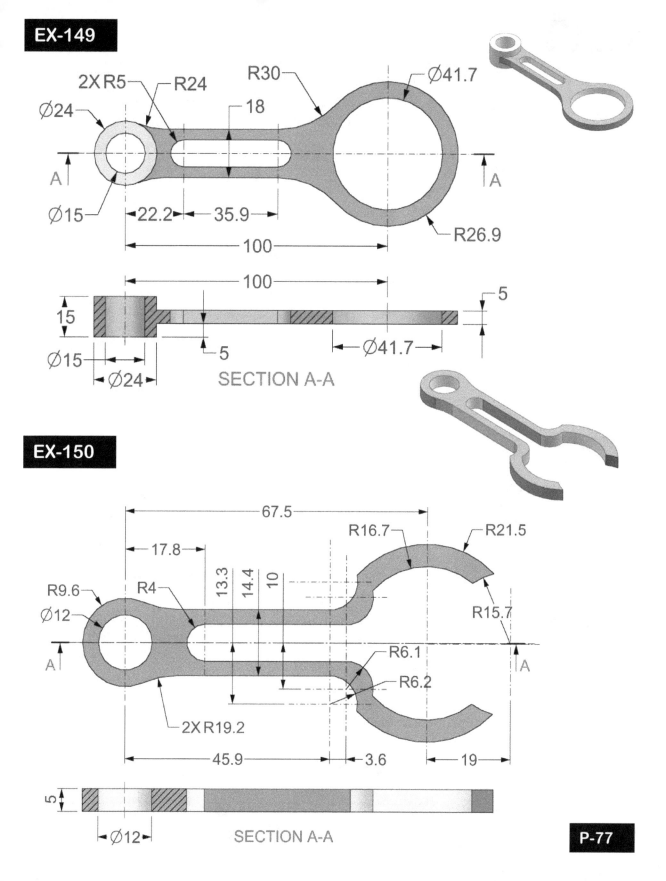

EX-149

2X R5 — R24   R30   Ø41.7

Ø24

18

R5

Ø15

A

22.2   35.9

100

R26.9

100

15   5

Ø15   5   Ø41.7

Ø24   SECTION A-A

EX-150

67.5

17.8   R16.7   R21.5

R9.6   R4   13.3   14.4   10

Ø12   R15.7

A   R6.1   A

R6.2

2X R19.2

45.9   3.6   19

5

Ø12   SECTION A-A

P-77

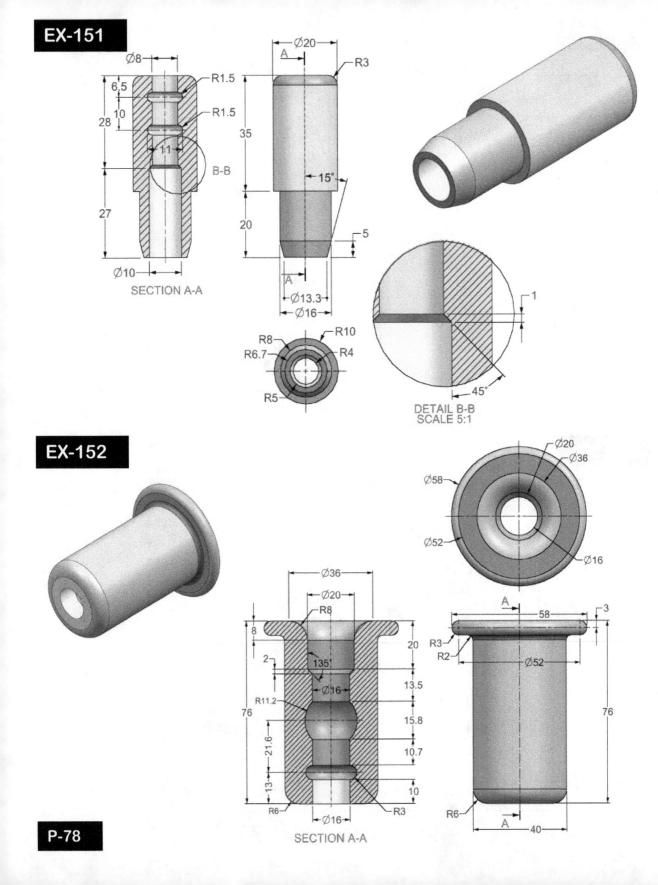

EX-151

Ø8
6,5
10
28
R1.5
R1.5
11
B-B
27
Ø10
SECTION A-A

Ø20
A
R3
35
15°
20
5
A
Ø13.3
Ø16

R8
R10
R6.7
R4
R5

1
45°
DETAIL B-B
SCALE 5:1

EX-152

Ø20
Ø36
Ø58
Ø52
Ø16

Ø36
Ø20
R8
8
2
135°
Ø16
R11.2
76
21.6
15.8
10.7
13
10
R6
R3
Ø16
SECTION A-A

20
13.5

A
58
3
R3
R2
Ø52
76
R6
A
40

P-78

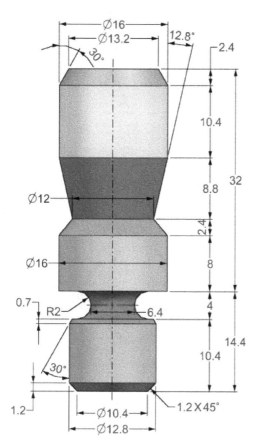

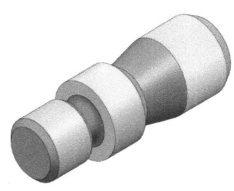

Ø16
Ø13.2
12.8°
2.4
30°
10.4
32
8.8
Ø12
2.4
Ø16
8
4
0.7
R2
6.4
14.4
30°
10.4
1.2
Ø10.4
1.2 X 45°
Ø12.8

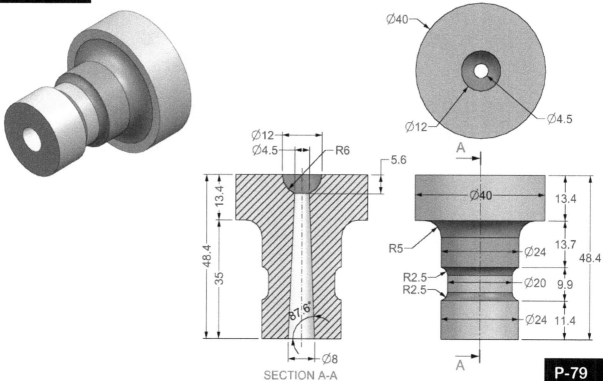

Ø40
Ø12
Ø4.5

Ø12
Ø4.5
R6
5.6
13.4
48.4
35
87.6°
Ø8
SECTION A-A

A
Ø40
13.4
R5
13.7
Ø24
R2.5
48.4
Ø20
9.9
R2.5
Ø24
11.4
A

EX-155

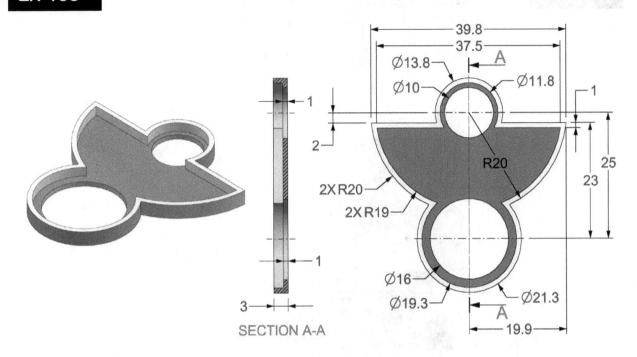

SECTION A-A

Ø13.8
Ø10
Ø11.8
39.8
37.5
A
1
2
25
23
R20
2X R20
2X R19
Ø16
Ø19.3
Ø21.3
19.9
1
3

EX-156

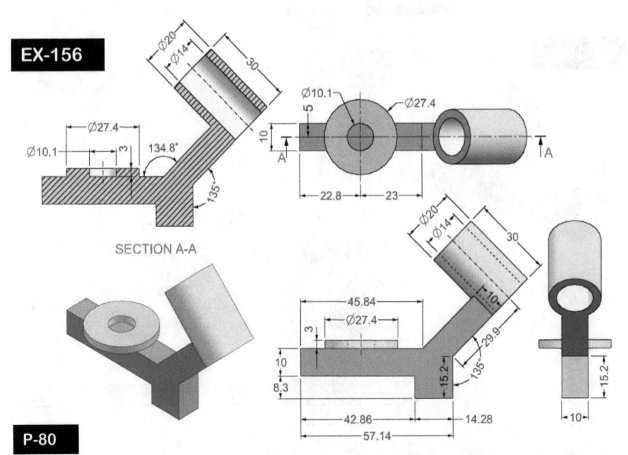

SECTION A-A

Ø20
Ø14
30
Ø27.4
Ø10.1
3
134.8°
135°

Ø10.1
Ø27.4
5
10
A
A
22.8
23

45.84
Ø27.4
3
10
8.3
42.86
57.14
14.28
Ø20
Ø14
30
10
29.9
135°
15.2
15.2
10

P-80

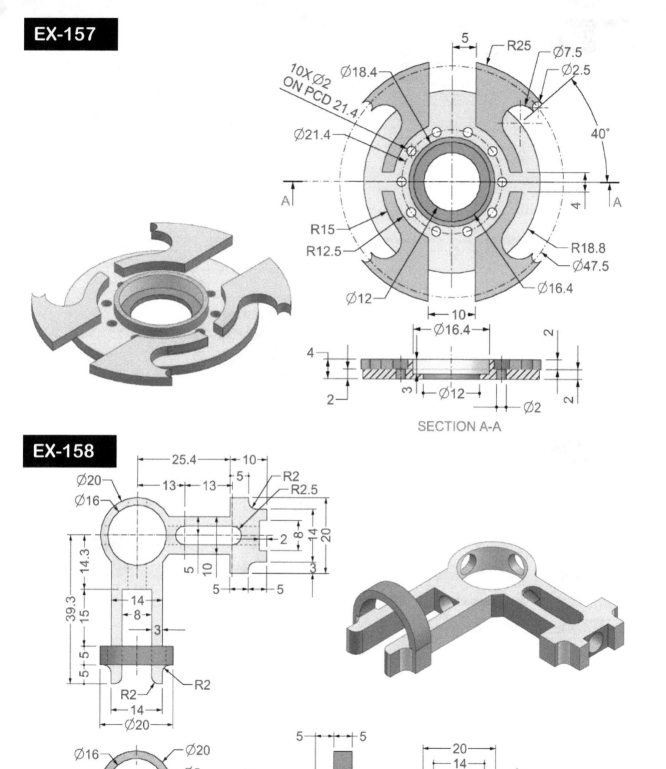

EX-157

10X Ø2
ON PCD 21.4

Ø18.4

Ø21.4

5

R25

Ø7.5

Ø2.5

40°

R15
R12.5

4

R18.8
Ø47.5

Ø12

Ø16.4

10

A

A

Ø16.4

4

2

2

3

Ø12

Ø2

2

SECTION A-A

EX-158

25.4

10

13

13

5

R2
R2.5

Ø20
Ø16

2

8

14

20

14.3

5

10

3

39.3

15

5

5

14

8

3

5

5

5+5

R2

R2

14

Ø20

Ø16

Ø20

Ø5

10

3

10

35.4

+5+5

6

5

5

20

14

7

Ø5

6

6

39.3

10

3

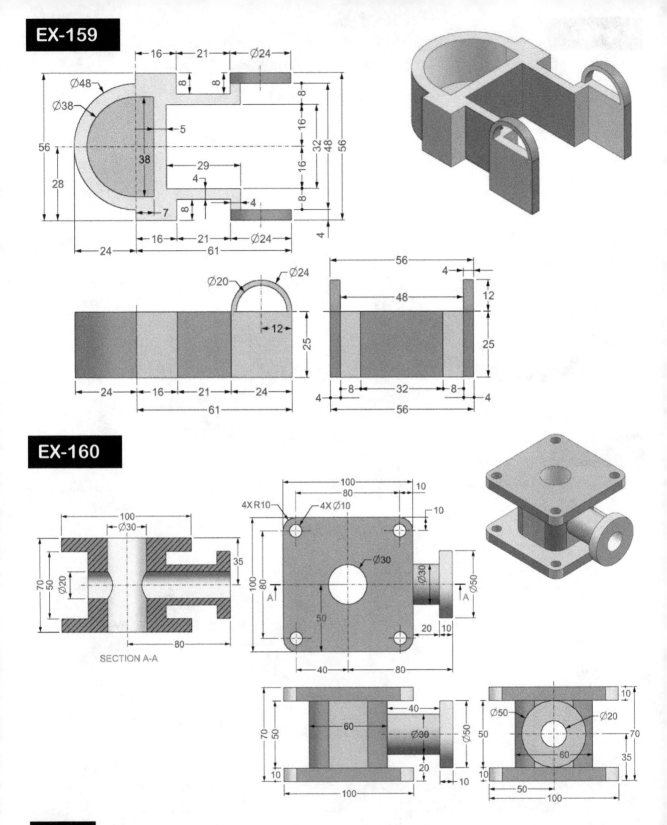

EX-159

EX-160

SECTION A-A

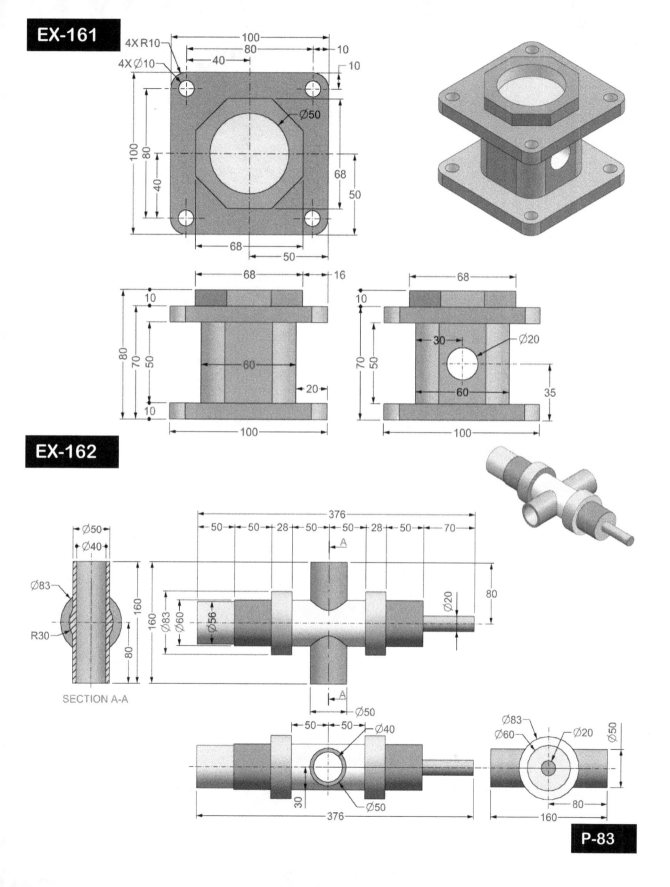

EX-161

4X R10
4X Ø10
100
80
40
10
10
100
80
40
Ø50
68
50
68
50

68
16
10
80
70
50
60
10
20
100

68
10
70
50
30
Ø20
60
35
100

EX-162

376
50
50
28
50
50
28
50
70
A

Ø50
Ø40
Ø83
R30
160
160
80
Ø83
Ø60
Ø56
Ø20
80
SECTION A-A
A

Ø50
50
50
Ø40
30
Ø50
376

Ø83
Ø60
Ø20
Ø50
80
160

P-83

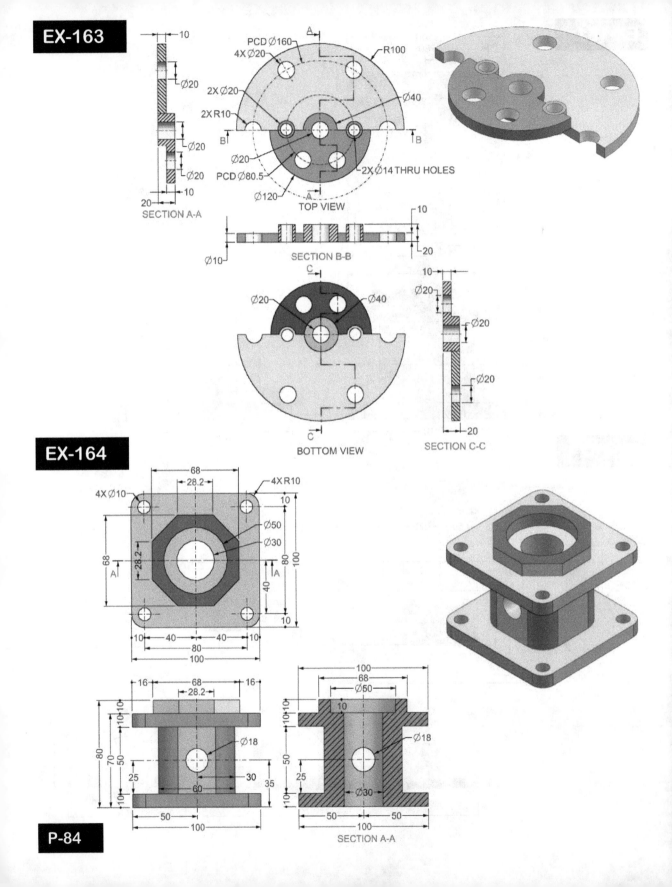

EX-163

PCD Ø160
4X Ø20
2X Ø20
2X R10
Ø20
PCD Ø80.5
Ø120
R100
Ø40
2X Ø14 THRU HOLES
TOP VIEW

SECTION A-A

10
Ø20
Ø20
Ø20
20
10

Ø10
SECTION B-B
10
20

BOTTOM VIEW
Ø20
Ø40

SECTION C-C
10
Ø20
Ø20
Ø20
20

EX-164

68
28.2
4X Ø10
4X R10
10
Ø50
Ø30
68
28.2
A
A
80
40
100
10
10
40
40
10
80
100

16
68
16
28.2
10
10
80
70
50
25
10
Ø18
30
60
35
50
100

100
68
Ø50
10
10
10
50
25
10
Ø18
Ø30
50
50
100
SECTION A-A

P-84

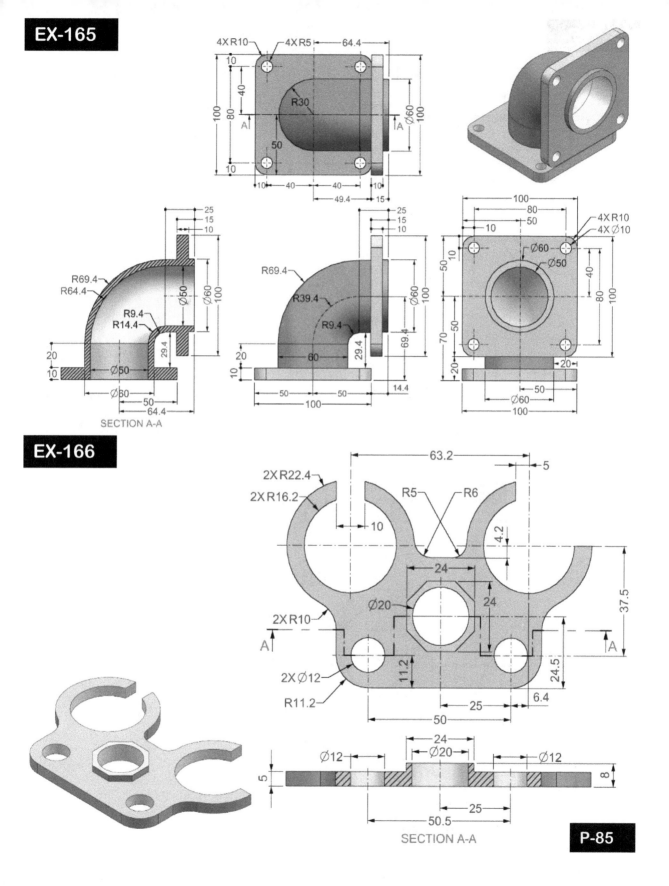

EX-165

4X R10   4X R5   64.4
10
40
80
100
R30
Ø60
100
A   A
50
10
10   40   40   10
49.4   15

25
15
10
R69.4
R64.4
Ø50
Ø60
100
R9.4
R14.4
29.4
20
10
Ø50
Ø60
50
64.4
SECTION A-A

25
15
10
R69.4
R39.4
Ø60
100
R9.4
69.4
29.4
20
60
10
14.4
50   50
100

100
80
50
4X R10
10
4X Ø10
Ø60
50
Ø50
50
10
40
80
100
70
50
20
20
50
Ø60
100

EX-166

2X R22.4
2X R16.2
R5   R6
63.2   5
10
4.2
24
Ø20
24
2X R10
A   A
11.2
37.5
2X Ø12
24.5
R11.2
6.4
25
50

24
Ø12   Ø20   Ø12
5   8
25
50.5
SECTION A-A

P-85

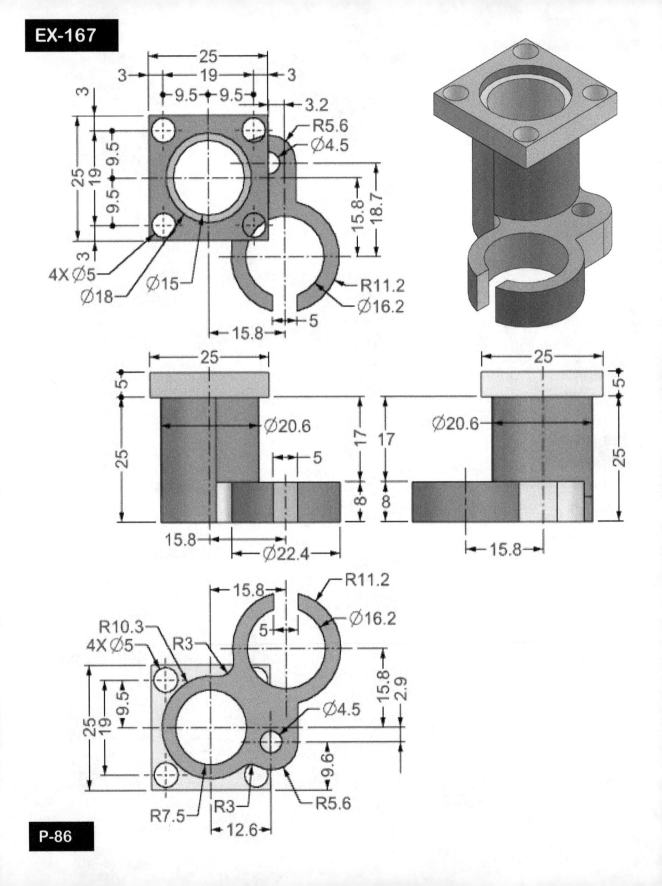

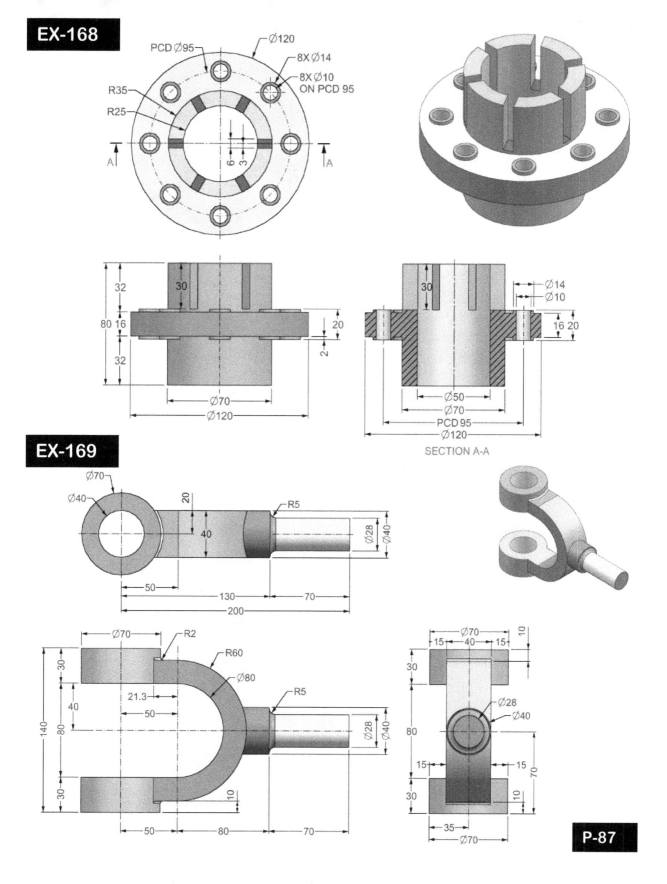

EX-168

PCD Ø95
Ø120
8X Ø14
8X Ø10
ON PCD 95
R35
R25

A

32
30
80 16
32
20
2
Ø70
Ø120

30
Ø14
Ø10
16 20
Ø50
Ø70
PCD 95
Ø120

SECTION A-A

EX-169

Ø70
Ø40
20
R5
40
Ø28
Ø40
50
130
70
200

Ø70
R2
R60
30
Ø80
R5
21.3
40
50
80
140
Ø28
Ø40
30
10
50
80
70

Ø70
15
40
15
10
30
Ø28
Ø40
80
70
15
15
30
10
35
Ø70

P-87

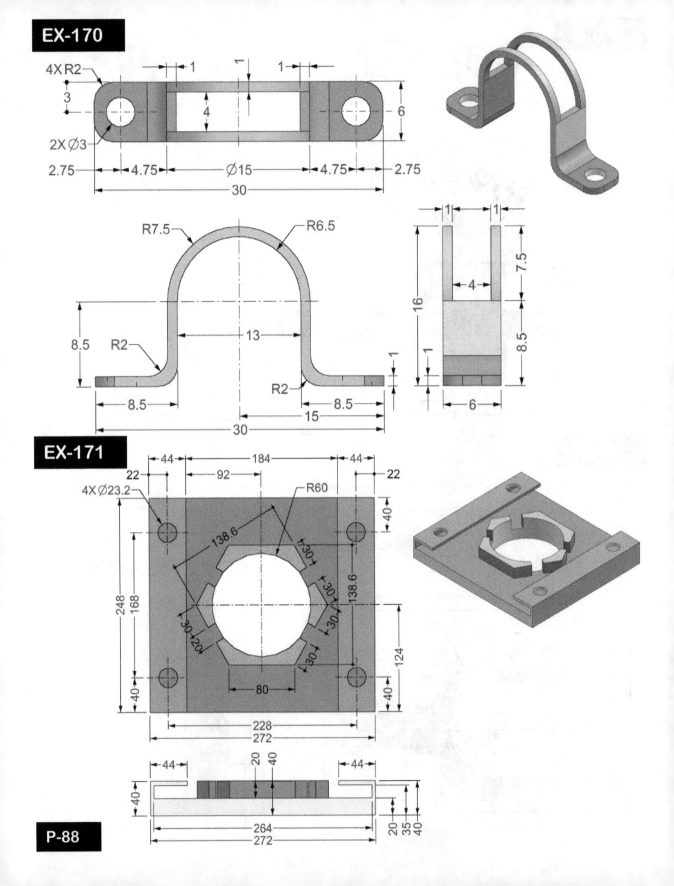

EX-170

4X R2
3
2X Ø3
2.75 4.75 Ø15 4.75 2.75
30
1 1 1
4
6

R7.5 R6.5
R2
8.5
13
R2
8.5 8.5
15
30

1 1
7.5
16
4
1 8.5
6

EX-171

44 184 44
22 92 22
4X Ø23.2
R60
138.6
30
30
30
30
248 168
138.6
30 20
30
124
80
40
40
228
272

44 20 40 44
40
264 20 35 40
272

P-88

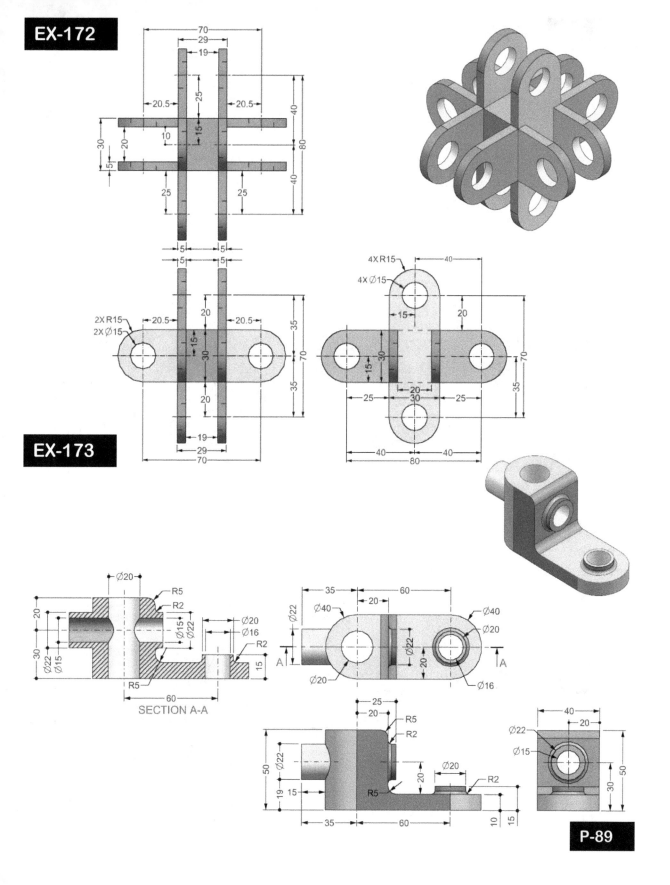

EX-172

EX-173

SECTION A-A

P-89

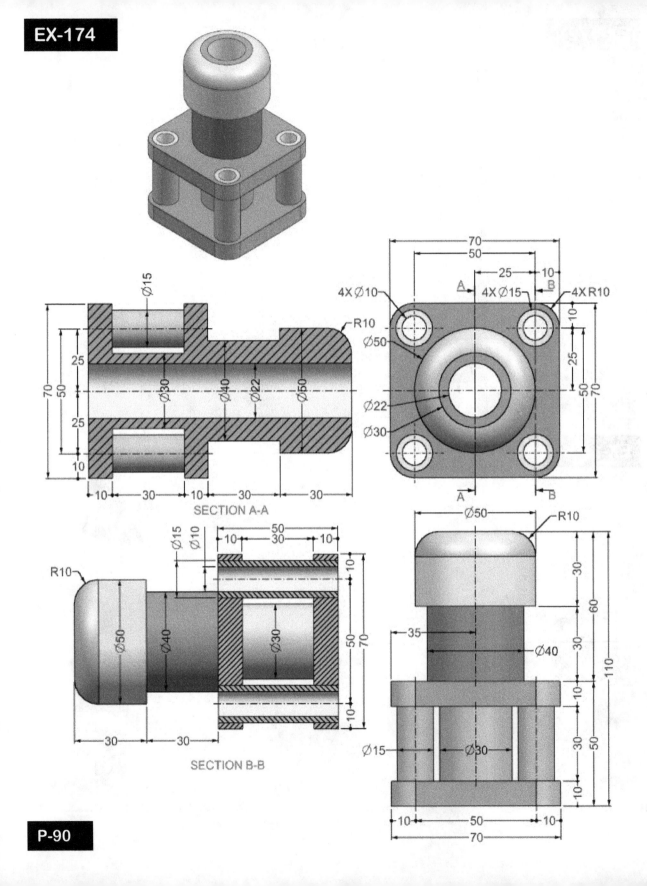

SECTION A-A

SECTION B-B

70
35 — 35
10 — 25 — 25 — 10 — 4X R10

4X Ø15
4X Ø10
Ø30
Ø22

10
35
25
70
25
35
10

A   A

Ø30
Ø15   Ø15
20
5
10
Ø15   Ø15
30
50
50
10
70

Ø30
Ø22
Ø15
Ø10
20
30
70
5
10
Ø22
30
10
25 — 25
50
70

SECTION A-A

EX-176

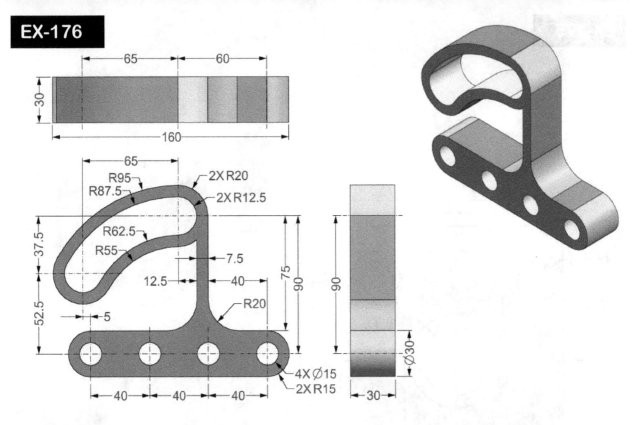

EX-177

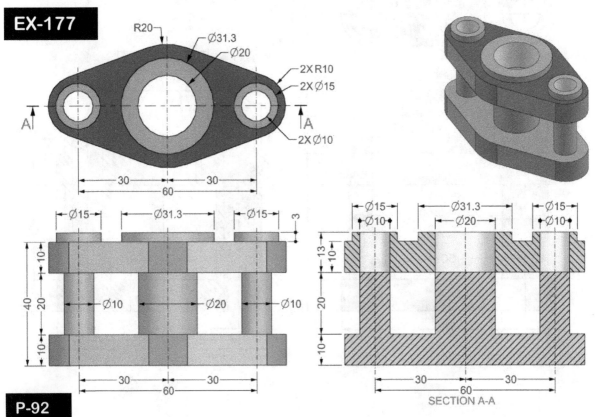

SECTION A-A

P-92

EX-178

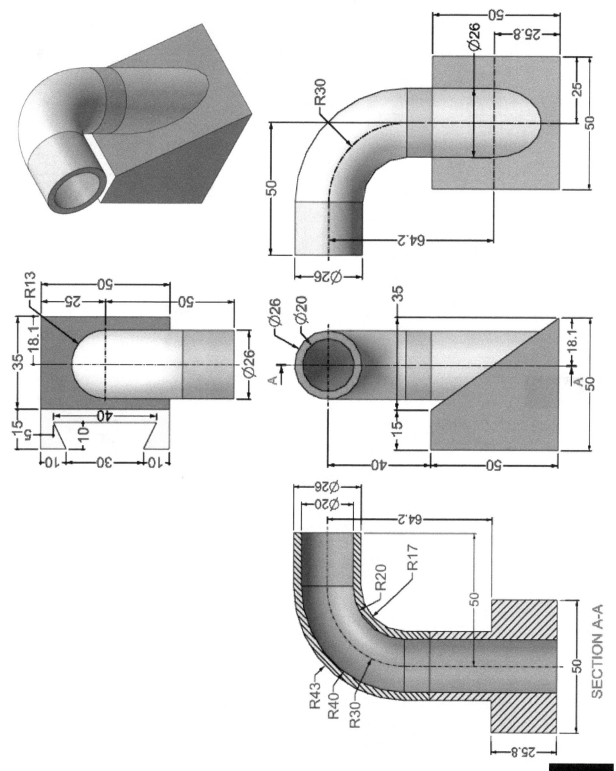

R30

∅26

50

25.8

25

50

64.2

∅26

R13

50

25

50

∅26

35

18.1

40

15

5

10

30

10

∅26
∅20

A

35

18.1

A

15

50

40

50

∅26
∅20

64.2

R20

R17

50

R43
R40
R30

50

25.8

SECTION A-A

P-93

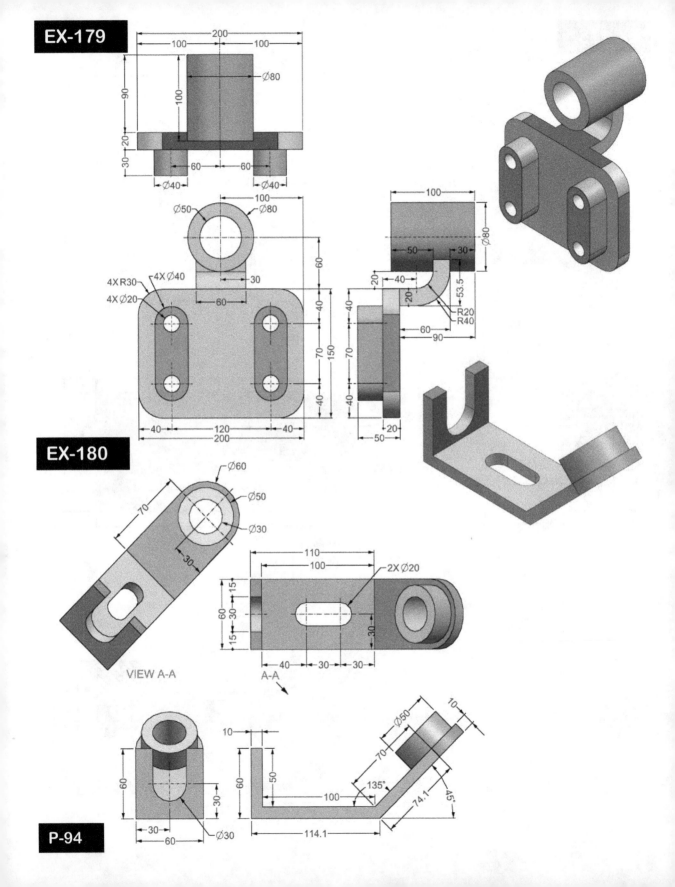

EX-179

Ø80
200
100
100
90
100
20
30
60
60
Ø40
Ø40

Ø50
Ø80
100
30
60
60
4X R30
4X Ø40
4X Ø20
40
70
150
60
40
40
40
120
40
200

100
50
30
Ø80
20
40
20
53.5
R20
R40
60
90
70
40
40
20
50

EX-180

Ø60
Ø50
70
30
Ø30

110
100
2X Ø20
15
30
15
60
30
40
30
30
A-A

VIEW A-A

P-94

60
30
30
Ø30
30
60

10
10
Ø50
70
60
50
135°
100
74.1
45°
114.1

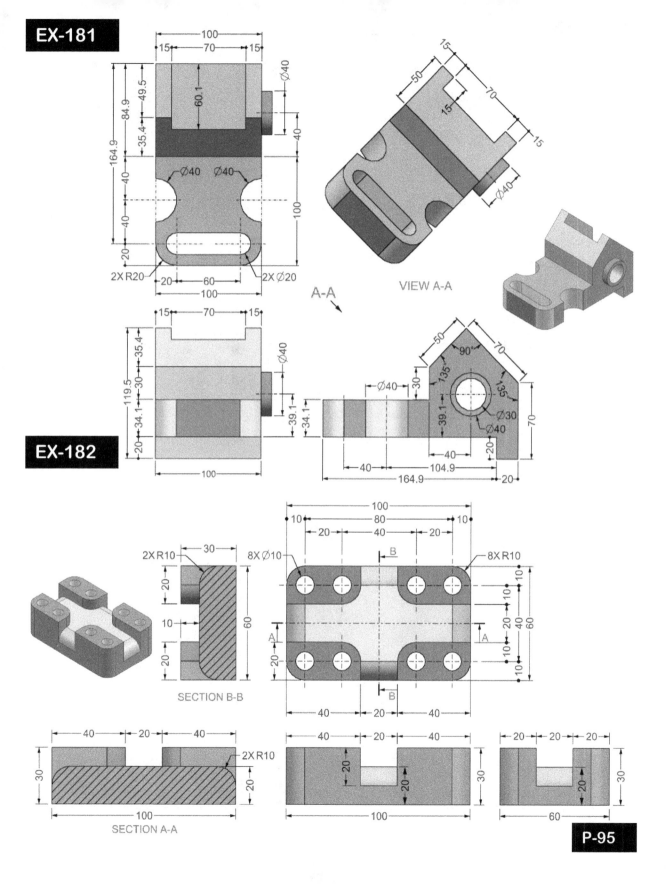

EX-181

EX-182

A-A

VIEW A-A

SECTION B-B

SECTION A-A

P-95

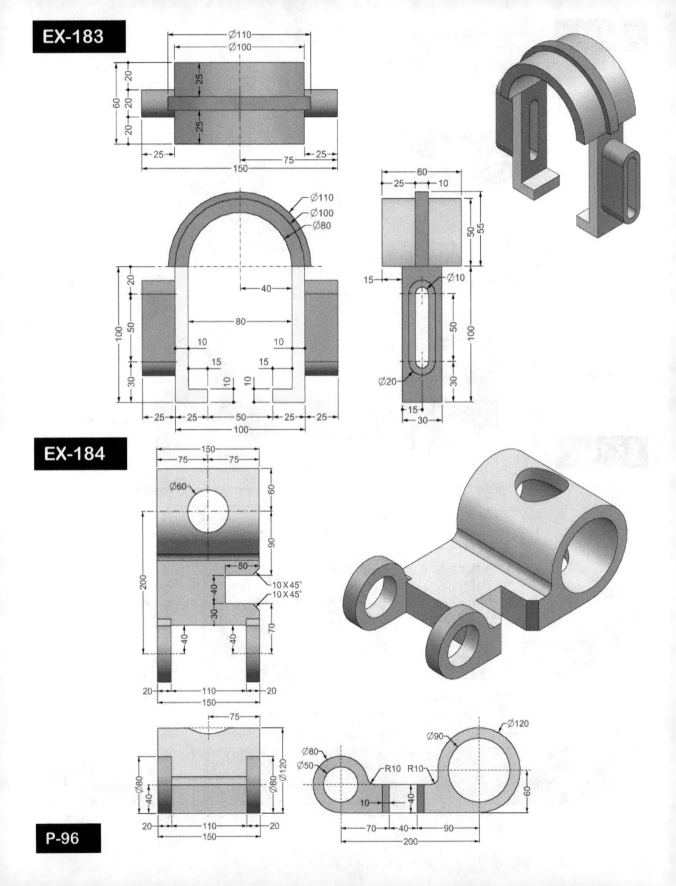

EX-183

Ø110
Ø100
20
20
60
20
25
25
25
25
75
150

Ø110
Ø100
Ø80
20
100
50
40
80
30
10   10
15   15
10   10
25 25 50 25 25
100

60
25   10
50
55
15
Ø10
50
100
30
Ø20
15
30

EX-184

150
75   75
Ø60
60
90
200
50
10 X 45°
40
30
10 X 45°
70
40   40
20   110   20
150

75
Ø80
Ø120
40
Ø80
20   110   20
150

Ø80
Ø50
Ø90
Ø120
R10 R10
10
40
60
70   40   90
200

P-96

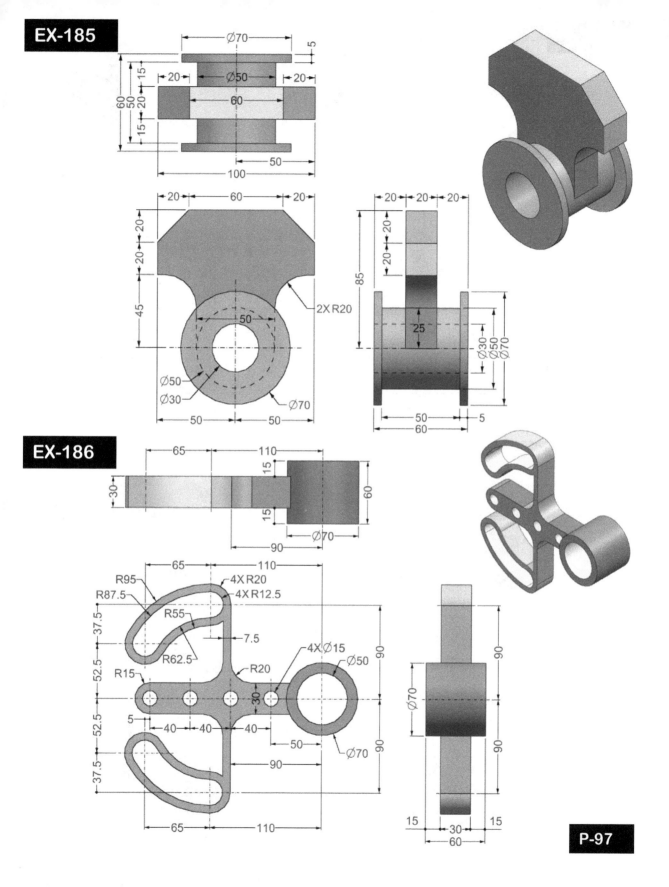

EX-185

Ø70
5
15
20
Ø50
20
60
50
20
60
15
50
100

20
60
20
20
20
45
50
2X R20
Ø50
Ø30
Ø70
50
50

20
20
20
85
20
20
25
Ø30
Ø50
Ø70
50
5
60

EX-186

65
110
15
30
15
Ø70
90

65
110
R95
4X R20
R87.5
4X R12.5
37.5
R55
7.5
52.5
R62.5
4X Ø15
Ø50
R15
R20
30
5
40
40
40
52.5
50
90
37.5
Ø70
65
110
90

90
Ø70
90
15
30
15
60

P-97

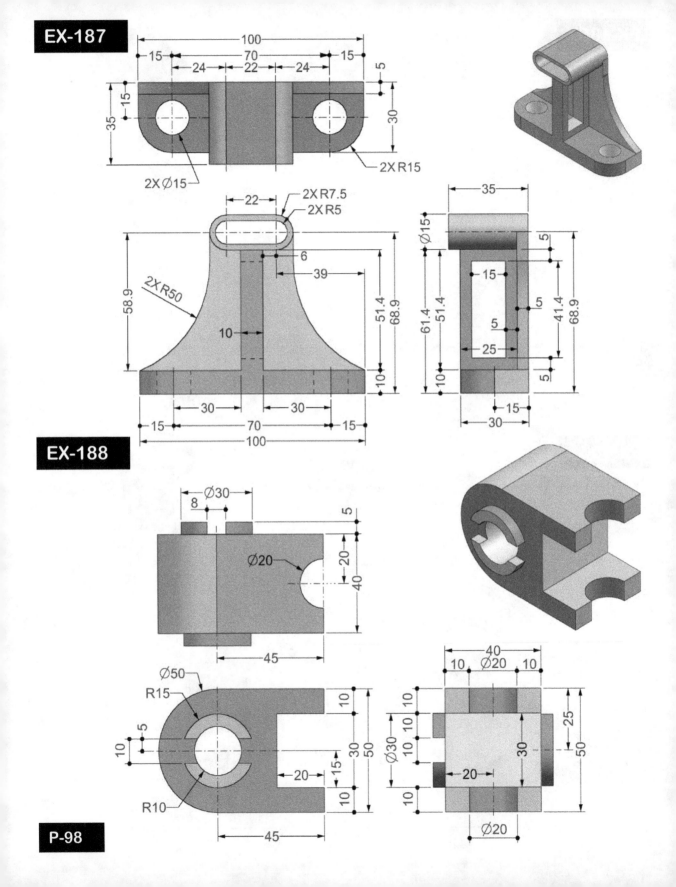

EX-187

100
15 · 70 · 15
24 · 22 · 24
5
15
35
30
2X R15
2X Ø15

2X R7.5
2X R5
22
6
39
58.9
2X R50
10
51.4
68.9
10
30 · 30
15 · 70 · 15
100

35
Ø15
5
15
5
61.4
51.4
5
41.4
68.9
25
5
10
15
30

EX-188

Ø30
8
5
20
40
Ø20
45

Ø50
R15
5
10
10
30
50
15
20
10
R10
45

40
10 Ø20 10
10
Ø30 10
25
10
50
30
20
10
Ø20

P-98

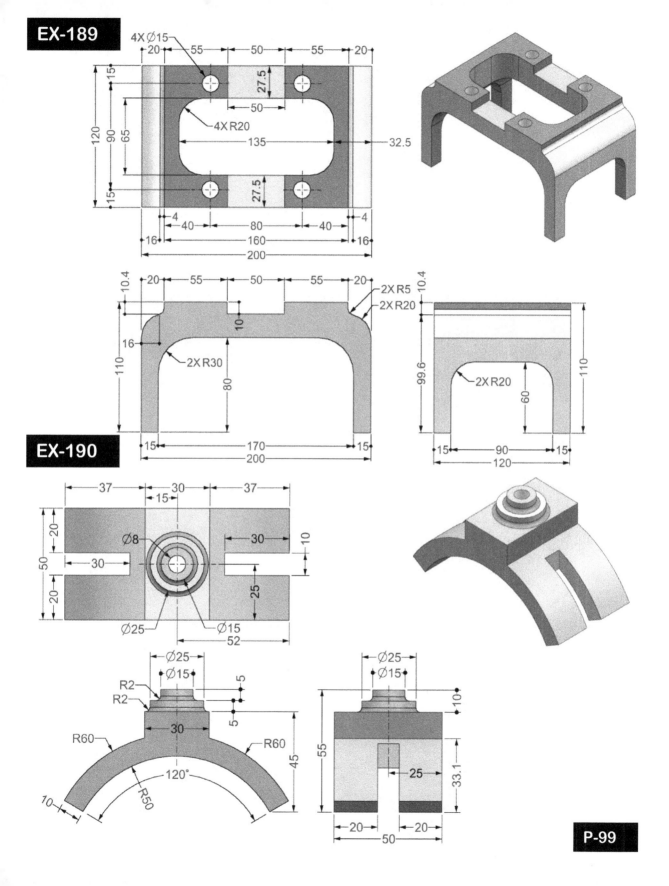

EX-189

4X Ø15
20 · 55 · 50 · 55 · 20
15
120
90
65
4X R20
27.5
50
135
32.5
27.5
15
4
40 · 80 · 40 · 4
16 · 160 · 16
200

10.4
20 · 55 · 50 · 55 · 20
2X R5
2X R20
16
10
110
2X R30
80
99.6
2X R20
60
110
15 · 170 · 15
200
15 · 90 · 15
120

EX-190

37 · 30 · 37
15
20
Ø8
50
30
30
10
25
20
Ø25
Ø15
52

Ø25
Ø15
R2
5
R2
R60
30
R60
45
120°
R50
R50
10

Ø25
Ø15
10
55
25
33.1
20 · 20
50

P-99

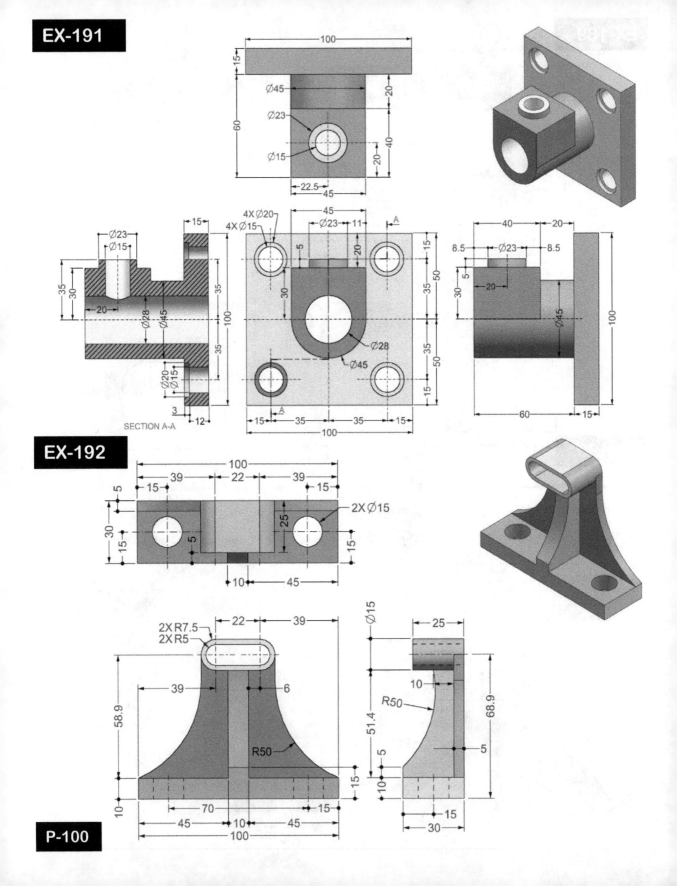

EX-191

SECTION A-A

4X Ø20
4X Ø15

Ø23

Ø28
Ø45

EX-192

2X Ø15

2X R7.5
2X R5

R50

R50

Ø15

P-100

EX-193

40
12
10
10
Ø20
Ø30
R2
80
60
1 x 45°
30
10
Ø8
Ø14

SECTION A-A

A
2X R10
2X Ø14
2X Ø8
R20
Ø30
15
40
30
60
30
10
Ø20
Ø30
55
A

Ø30
Ø23
R2
R2
Ø14
40
15
10
12
55

40
Ø30
Ø14
20
R3.2
40
10
12
30
30
60

EX-194

150
110
4X Ø20
20
55
20
20
40
40
R5
15
15
130
30
60
40
Ø120
30
40
70
35
40

ALL HOLES CHAMFER 2MM

130°
2X Ø20
2X Ø50
Ø120
25°
R5
75
80
PCD Ø160
Ø100
R5
40
R5
40
70
35
40

60
30
15
80
80
30
40
20
R5
20
40
130

70
50
4X Ø20
60
20
20
110
150
BOTTOM VIEW

P-101

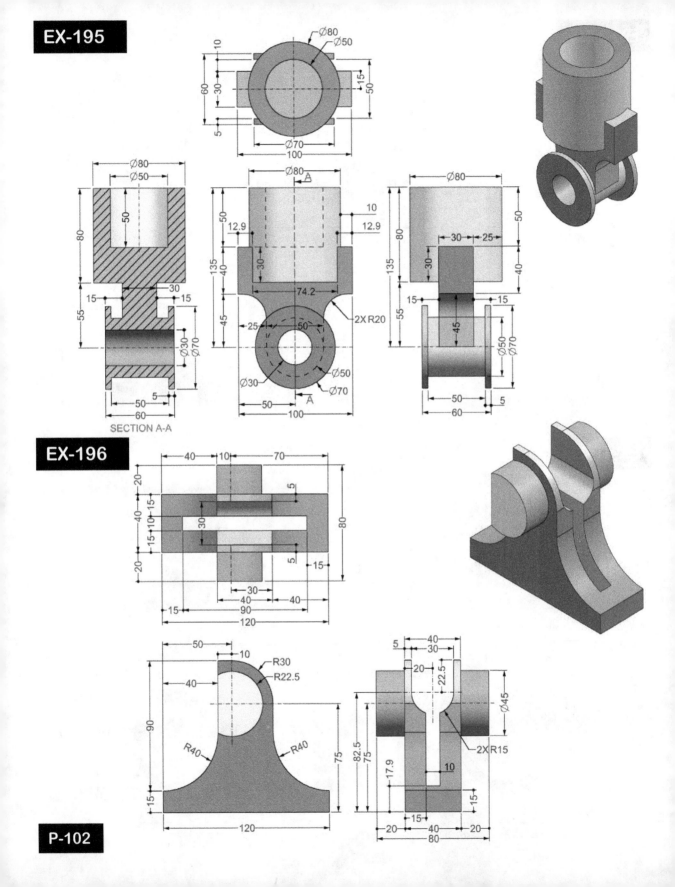

EX-195

Ø80
Ø50
10
60
30
15
50
5
Ø70
100

Ø80
Ø50
50
80
15
30
15
Ø30
Ø70
55
5
50
60
SECTION A-A

Ø80
A
50
12.9
135
30
40
74.2
45
25
50
2X R20
Ø30
Ø50
Ø70
50
100
A
10
12.9

Ø80
50
30
25
80
30
135
40
15
15
45
55
Ø50
Ø70
50
5
60

EX-196

40
10
70
20
5
40
15
10
15
80
30
15
20
5
15
30
40
40
15
90
120

50
10
R30
R22.5
40
90
R40
R40
75
15
120

5
40
30
20
22.5
Ø45
82.5
75
17.9
2X R15
10
15
15
20
40
20
80

P-102

EX-197

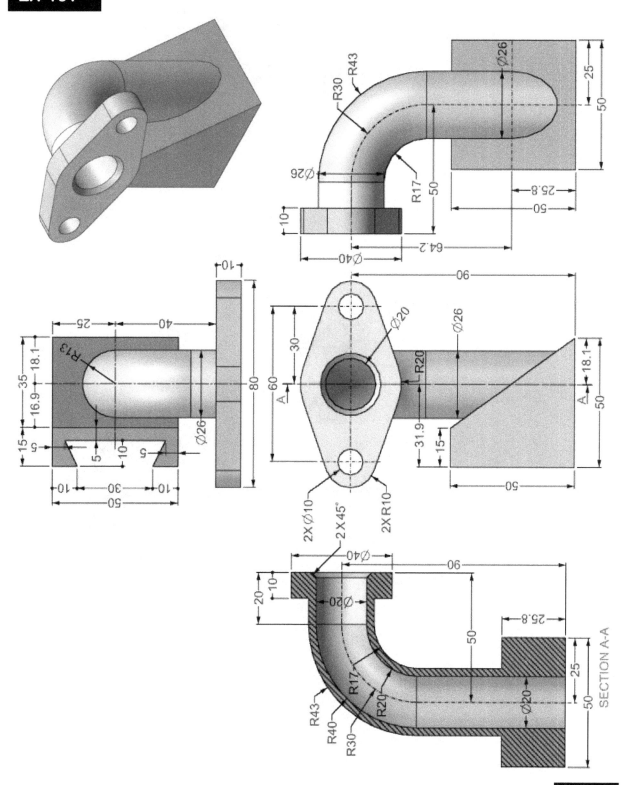

R43
R30
Ø26
25
50
50
25.8
Ø26
R17
50
64.2
Ø40
10

10
25
40
R13
35
18.1
16.9
80
Ø26
15
5
5
10
5
10
30
10
50

90
Ø20
30
60
A
Ø26
R20
A
18.1
31.9
50
15
50
2X Ø10
2X 45°
2XR10

Ø40
90
2X 45°
20
10
Ø20
25.8
50
25
R17
50
R43
R40
R30
R20
Ø20
50

SECTION A-A

P-103

6X Ø15THRU
ON PCD 90
Ø120
Ø50
Ø40
PCD Ø90

A
A

Ø120
Ø50
Ø40
15
10
Ø15
120
30
60°
80
Ø10
5
10
Ø20
Ø30
PCD 54

SECTION A-A

B-B

VIEW B-B

Ø20
8X Ø10THRU
ON PCD 54
Ø30
Ø70
PCD Ø54

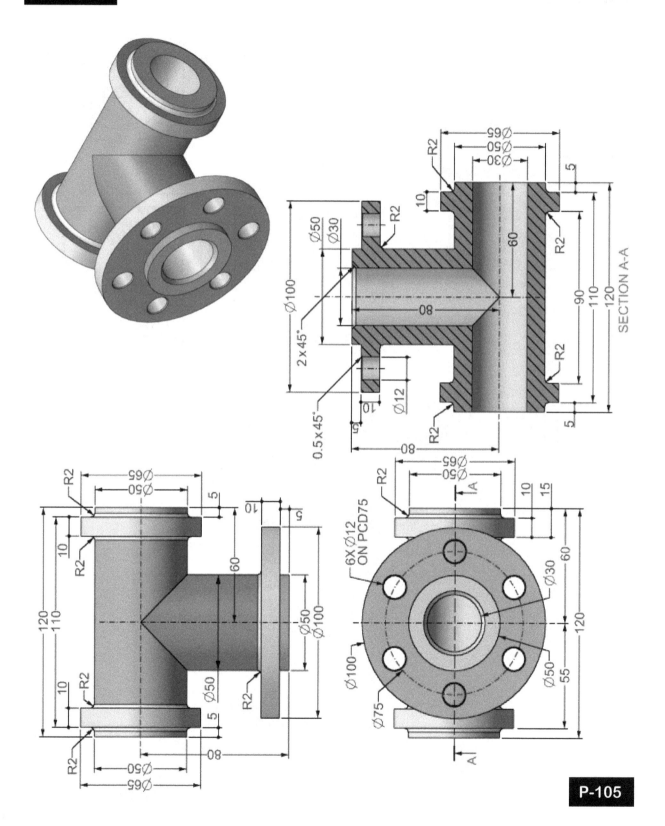

SECTION A-A

Ø65
Ø50
Ø30
R2
10
60
R2
90
110
120
5
R2
R2
5
80

Ø50
Ø30
R2
Ø100
2 x 45°
80
0.5x45°
Ø12
10
5
R2

R2
Ø65
Ø50
5
10
R2
120
110
60
Ø50
Ø100
10
R2
5
R2
80
Ø50
Ø65
R2

R2
Ø65
Ø50
A
10
15
6X Ø12
ON PCD75
60
Ø30
120
Ø100
Ø50
55
Ø75
A

EX-200

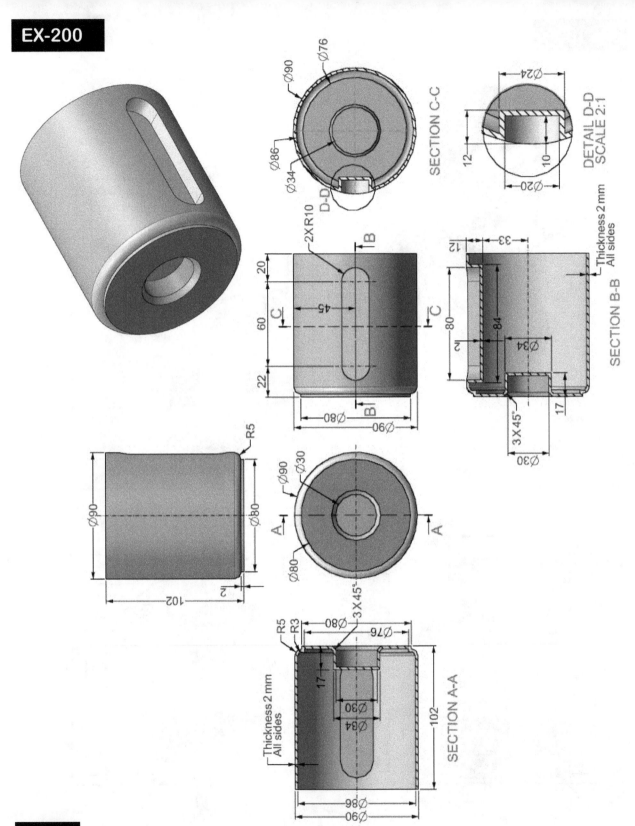

Ø90
Ø76
Ø86
Ø34
D-D
SECTION C-C

Ø24
12
10
Ø20
DETAIL D-D
SCALE 2:1
Thickness 2 mm
All sides

2XR10
20
B
C
45
60
C
22
B
Ø80
Ø90

12
33
80
Ø34
12
17
3×45°
Ø30
SECTION B-B
Thickness 2 mm
All sides

R5
Ø90
Ø80
2
102

Ø90
Ø30
A
A
Ø80

R5
R3
Ø80
3×45°
Ø76
17
Ø30
Ø84
102
Thickness 2 mm
All sides
Ø98
Ø90
SECTION A-A

P-106

Other useful books by CADIN360

1. 150 CAD Exercises

2. AutoCAD Exercises

3. CAD Exercises

4. 50+ SolidWorks Exercises

5. SolidWorks 200 Exercises

6. Autodesk Inventor Exercises

7. Catia Exercises

8. Siemens NX Exercises

©Copyright 2019 CADIN360, All rights reserved

www.ingramcontent.com/pod-product-compliance
Lightning Source LLC
Chambersburg PA
CBHW060448060326
40689CB00020B/4471

* 9 781072 019909 *